Weird & Whimsical
Coloring Book
FOR ADULTS by Roberto Sabas

Introduction & Tips

Thank you for buying this coloring book featuring weird, wacky, and whimsical art from my sketch books and October drawing sessions over the years. Inside are both line art and grayscale images for use with color pencil and color marker (or crayon if you don't have either of the first two items). With markers, place a backing sheet behind the page you are coloring to prevent any color bleed-through from marking the next image.

Opposite each image is an optional tip in light gray text to help you get optimal results—or perhaps you like to experiment, it's up to you!

My general suggestions are:

1. Decide which medium to use on an image and stick with it for that particular image.

2. If you want to mix media, try it out on a scrap sheet first to make sure they work well together.

3. Start on primary objects of the same general color scheme. Then work outward to smaller details. Once most of the image is colored, you can color in last the larger negative spaces (aka the background)—Or you can color the background and then finer details last.

4. Start with light strokes to build up layers of tone then go in with heavier strokes for a more opaque look where needed.

Note: this book and its entirety (i.e., all art images and the layout itself) are the property of Roberto F. V. Sabas. Additionally all images within this book and its cover are copyrighted ©2024 or earlier by Roberto Sabas, all rights reserved, however the purchaser of this book may photocopy page(s) for personal use or for testing out colors. etc. For any other usage, please ask author for permission to use: roberto.sabas@gmail.com. Thank you!

On the next page is the table of contents to each category of grouping and each individual page. Line art or grayscale is indicated for each page. Please enjoy coloring these images!

TABLE OF CONTENTS

* Below are the original gags—on page 103, have fun coloring in the pictures, write your own gag lines and (if you're up for it) send me scanned image of your work with your own gags to: roberto.sabas@gmail.com. Please do not send spam or personal requests, except as it pertains to copyright of this book or its content. Thank you for supporting me!

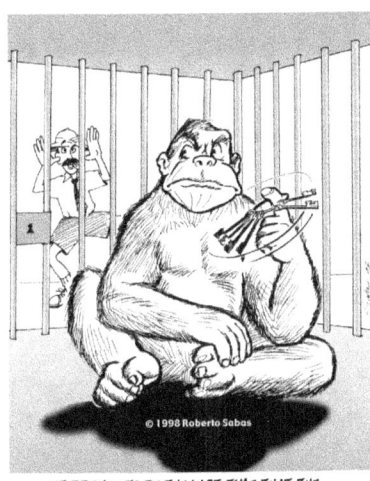

IT PROVED TO BE THE LAST TIME THAT THE ZOOKEEPER WOULD TAUNT LULU...

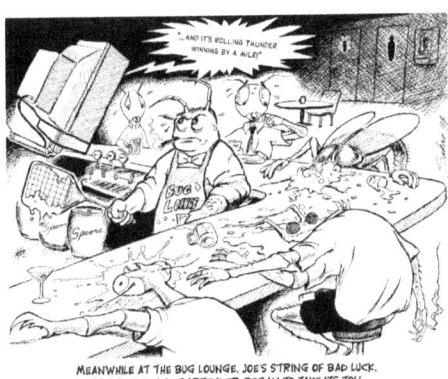

MEANWHILE AT THE BUG LOUNGE, JOE'S STRING OF BAD LUCK, AS A BOOKIE AND BARTENDER, BEGAN TO TAKE ITS TOLL.

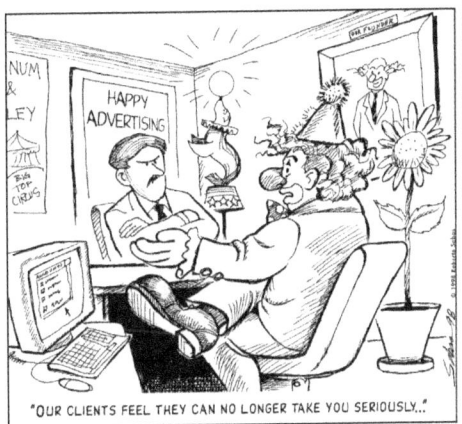

"OUR CLIENTS FEEL THEY CAN NO LONGER TAKE YOU SERIOUSLY..."

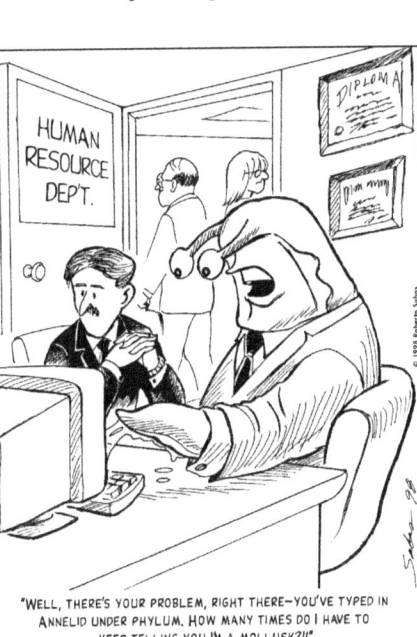

"WELL, THERE'S YOUR PROBLEM, RIGHT THERE—YOU'VE TYPED IN ANNELID UNDER PHYLUM. HOW MANY TIMES DO I HAVE TO KEEP TELLING YOU IM A MOLLUSK?!!"

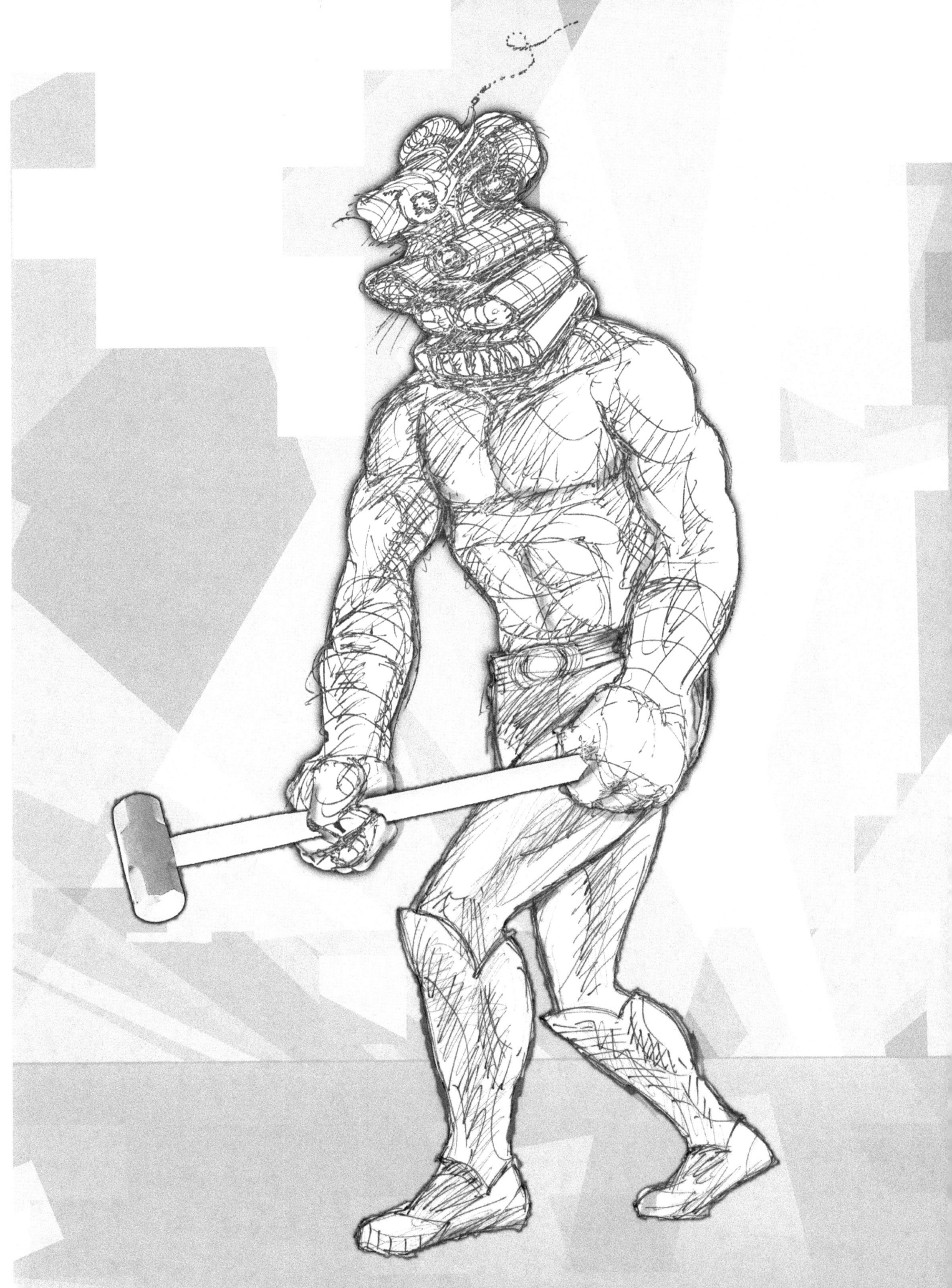

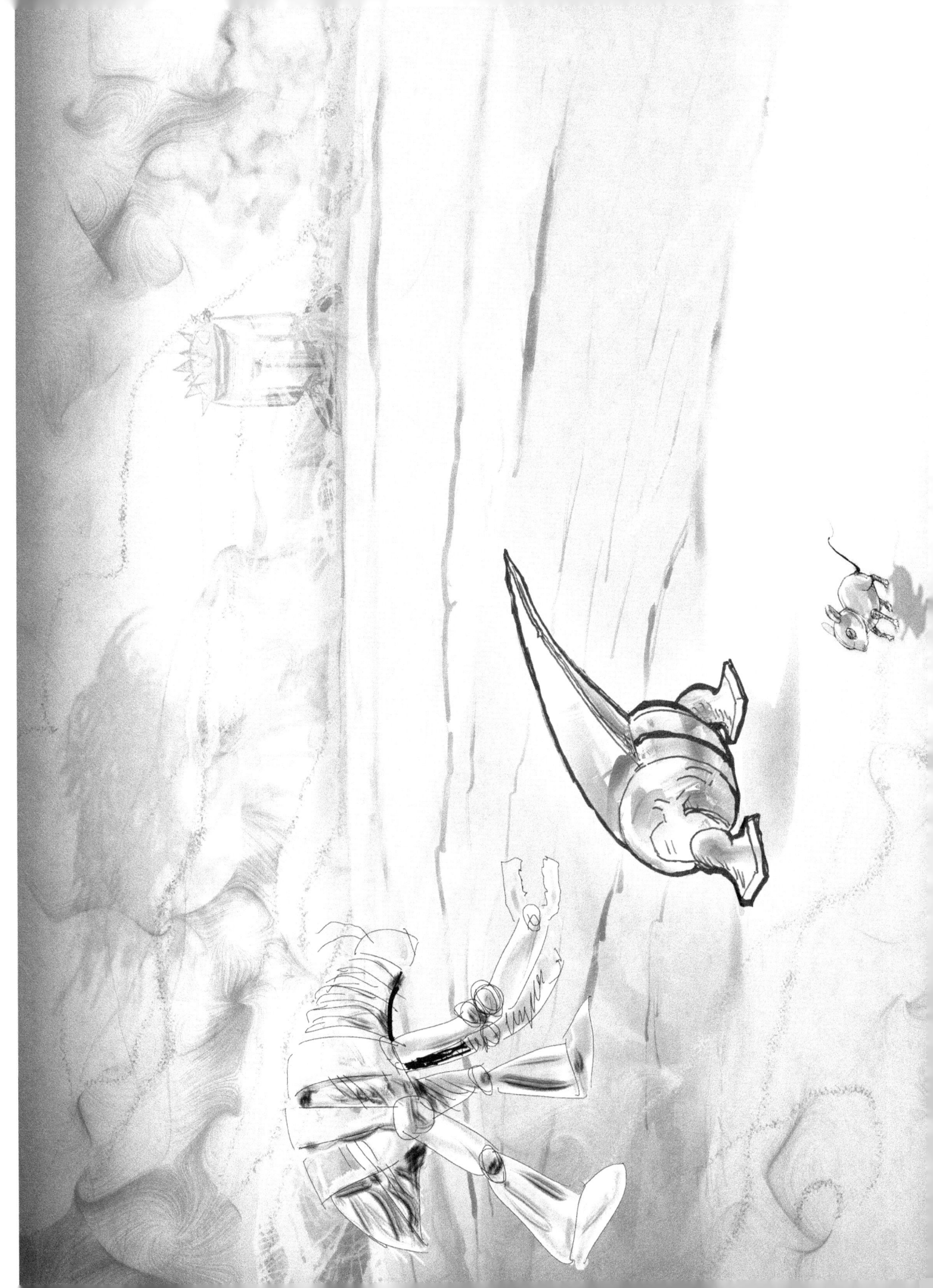

ARTIST'S TIP: Make a photocopy to test out your favorite color theme or color palette before coloring this or any other page that applies. It will be good practice for working on individual shapes within an intricate pattern.

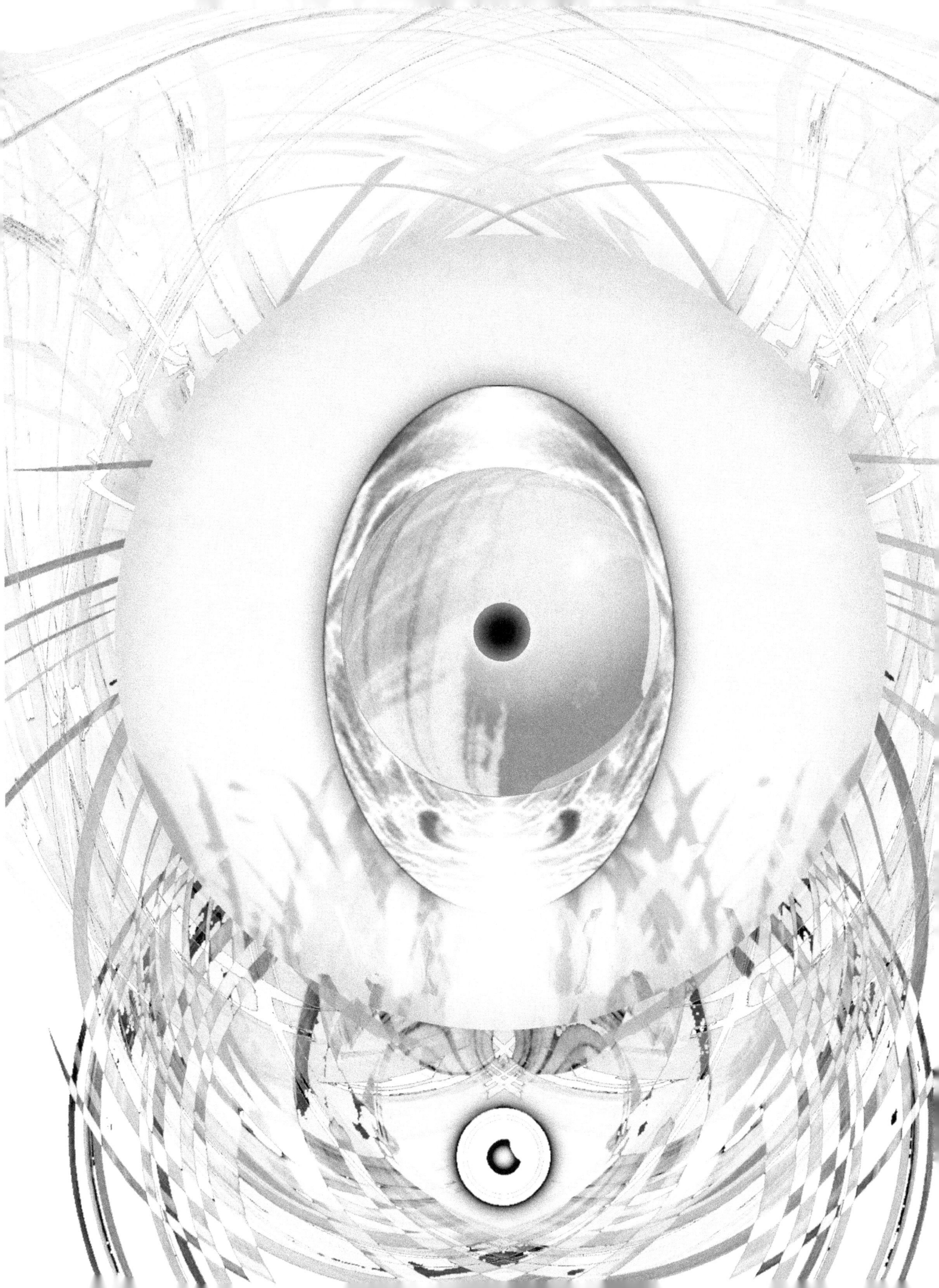

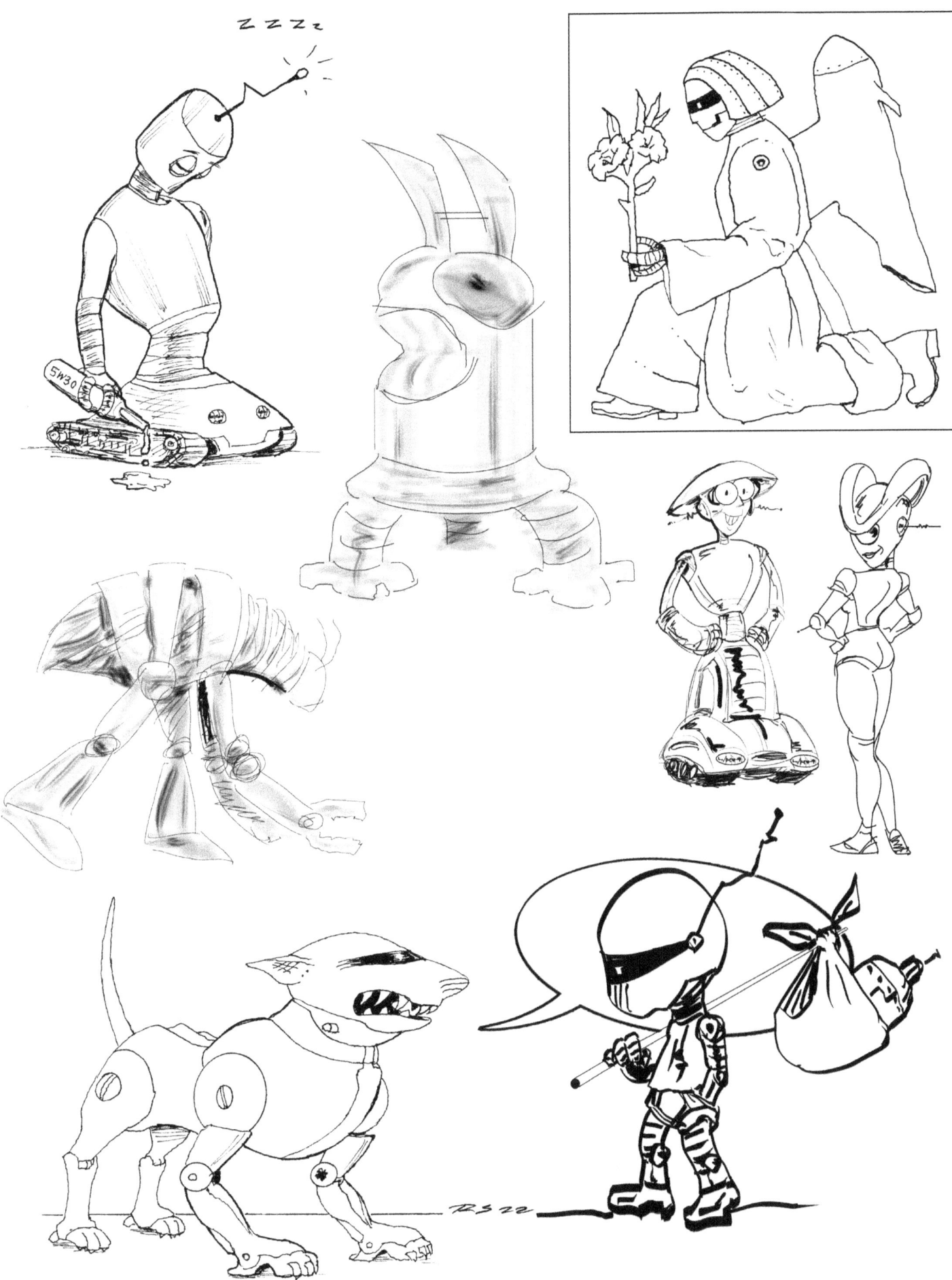

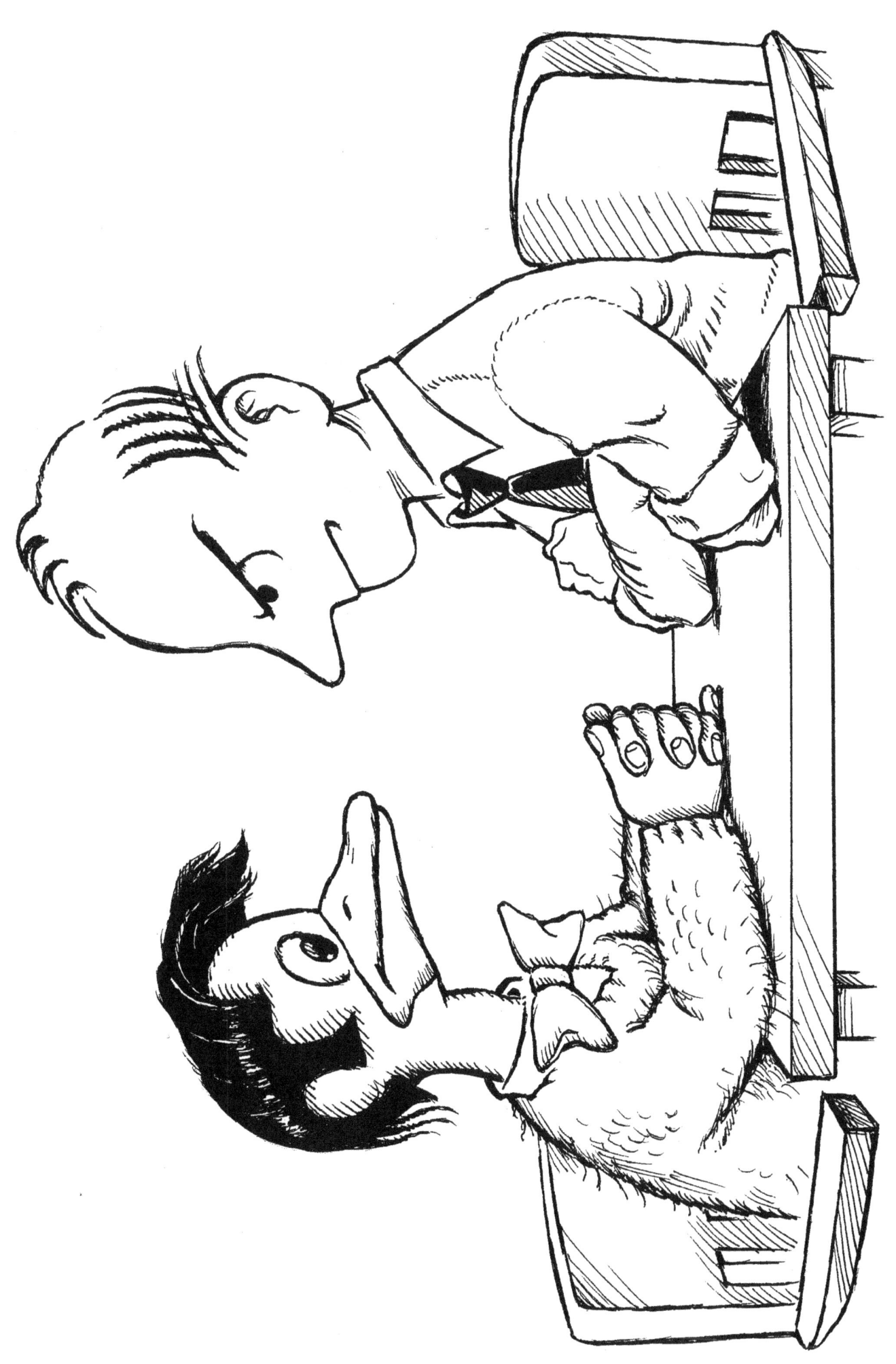

ARTIST'S TIP: For the bust of Poe, I recommend leaving that for last so that you can exploit the paper as the stone's color. Add in shade with a light blue. If you like, leave an uncolored halo around the statue that you can color in with a light hue like orange or yellow. For the raven's head, try using light purple and then build up the tone as you work out where the shady areas of its head will be. Don't overwork the framed portraits as they are tiny areas that only need a hint of tone to give a realistic feel as background elements.

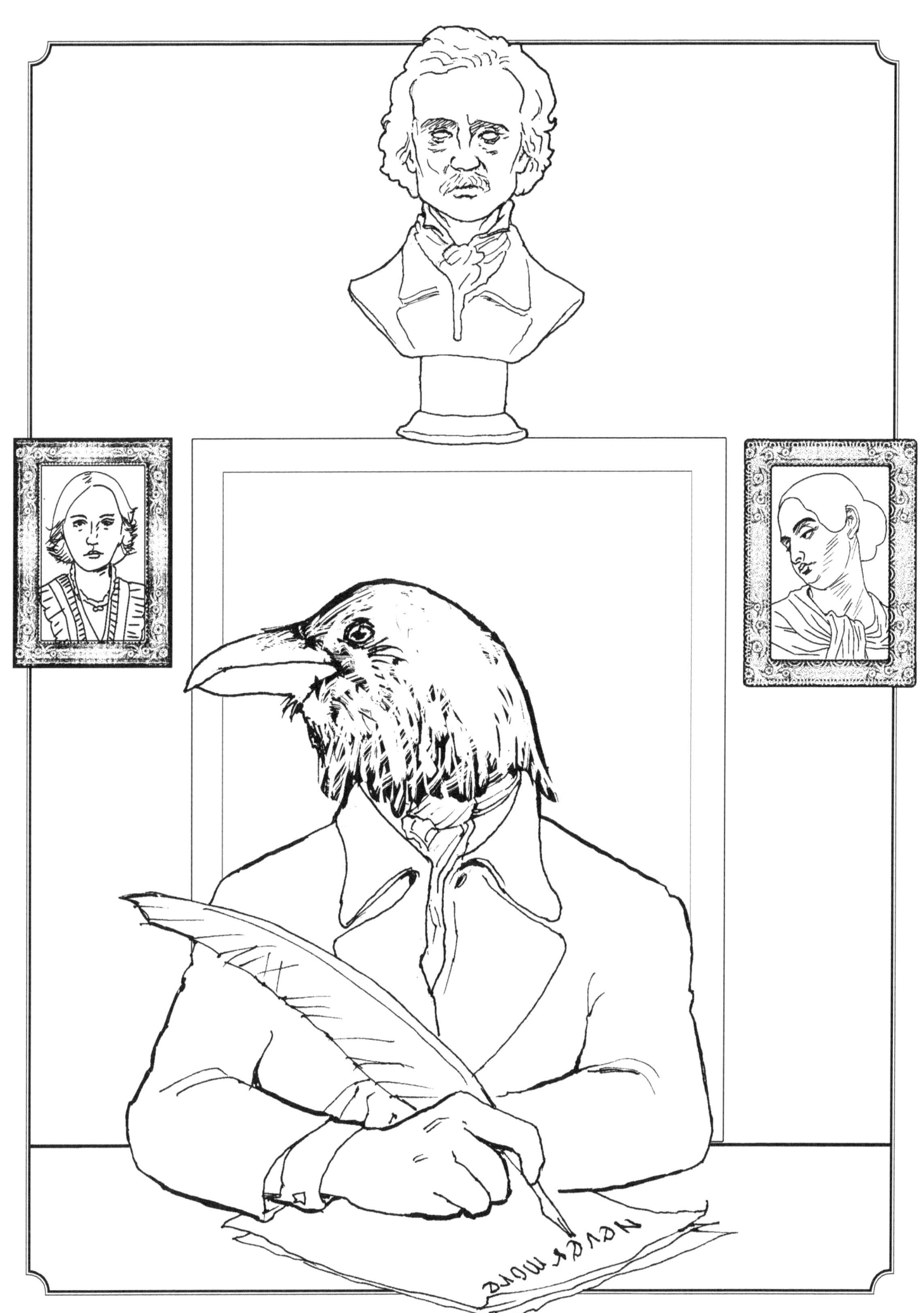

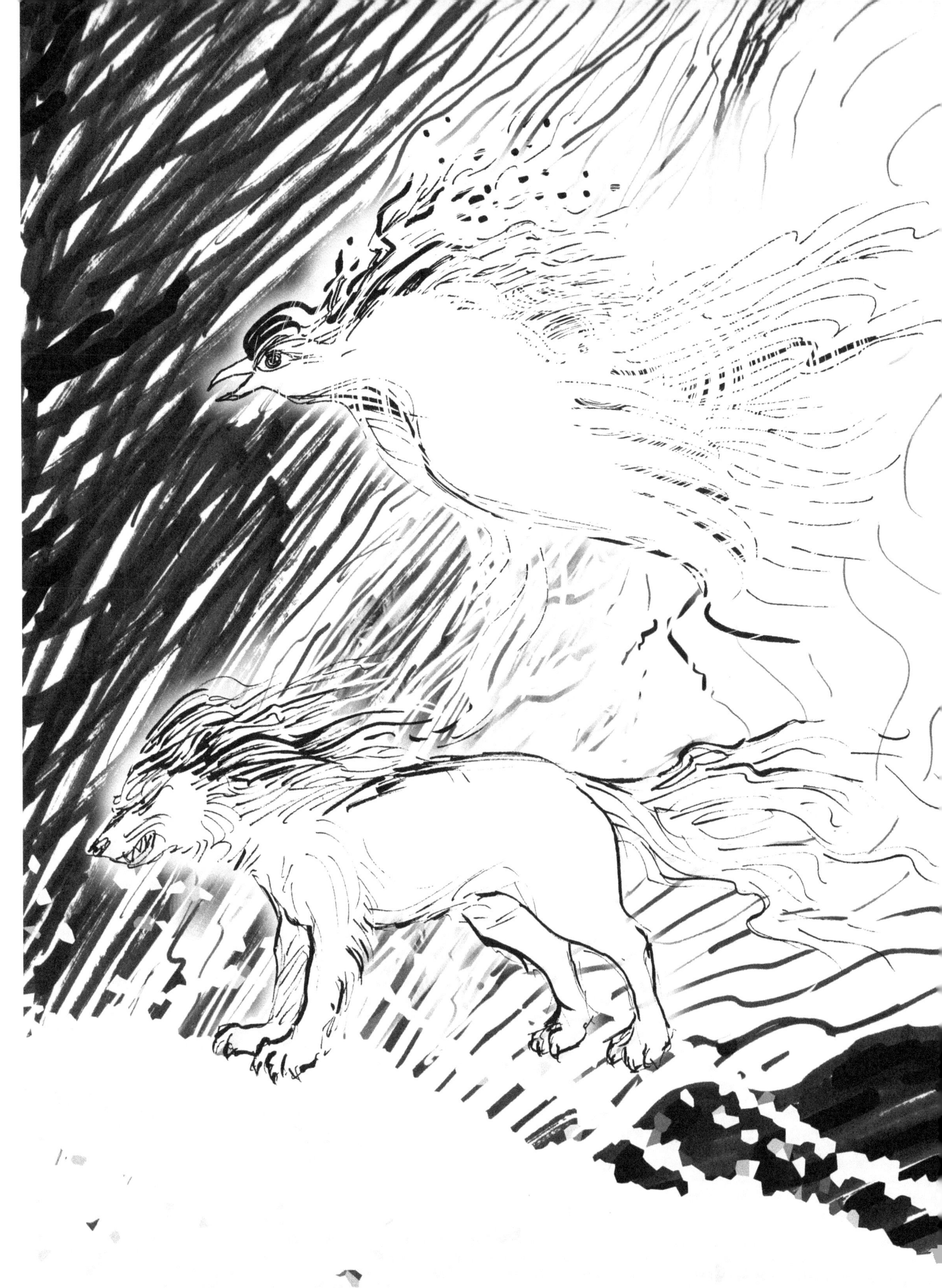

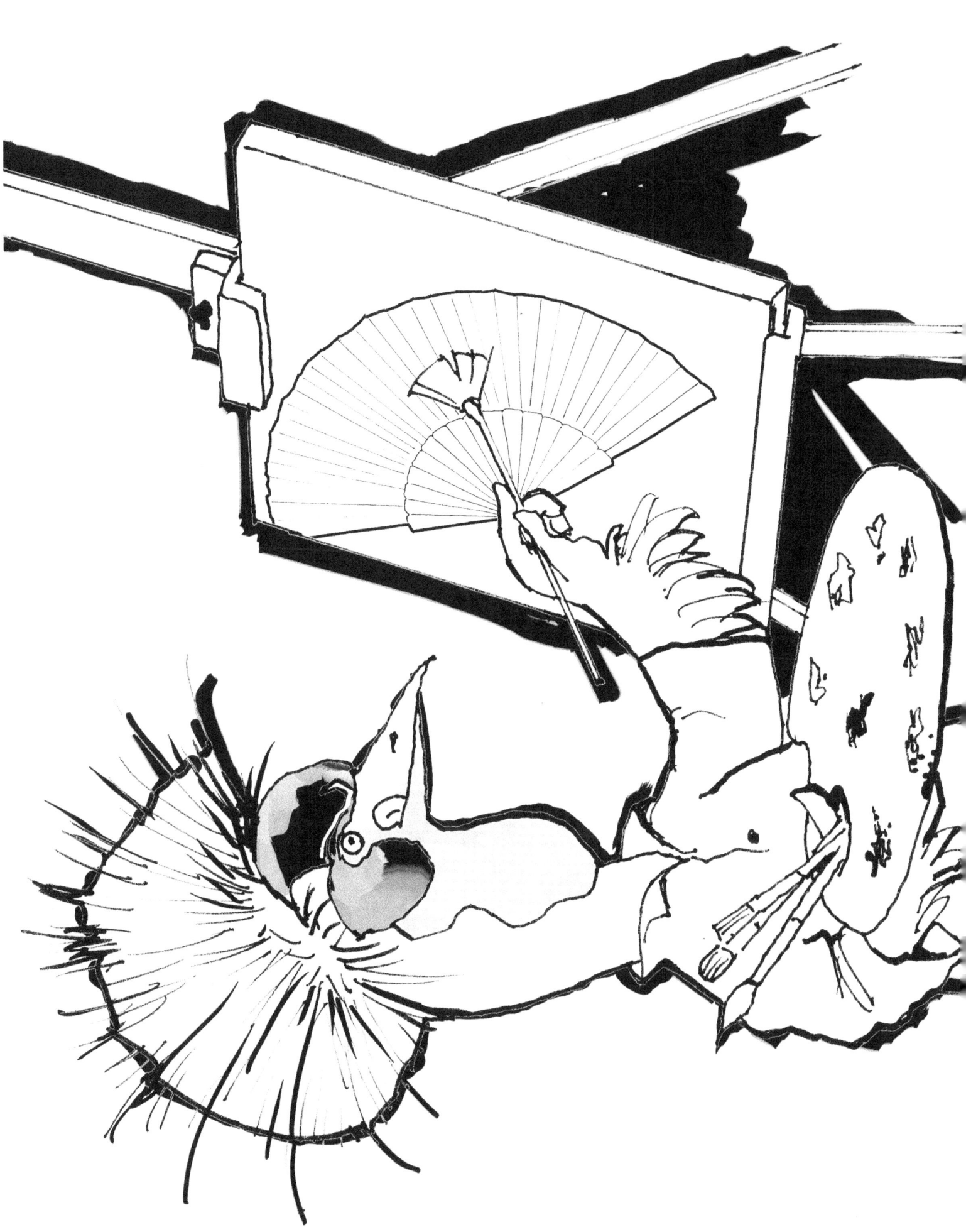

ARTIST'S TIP: Have fun inventing a background for this image!

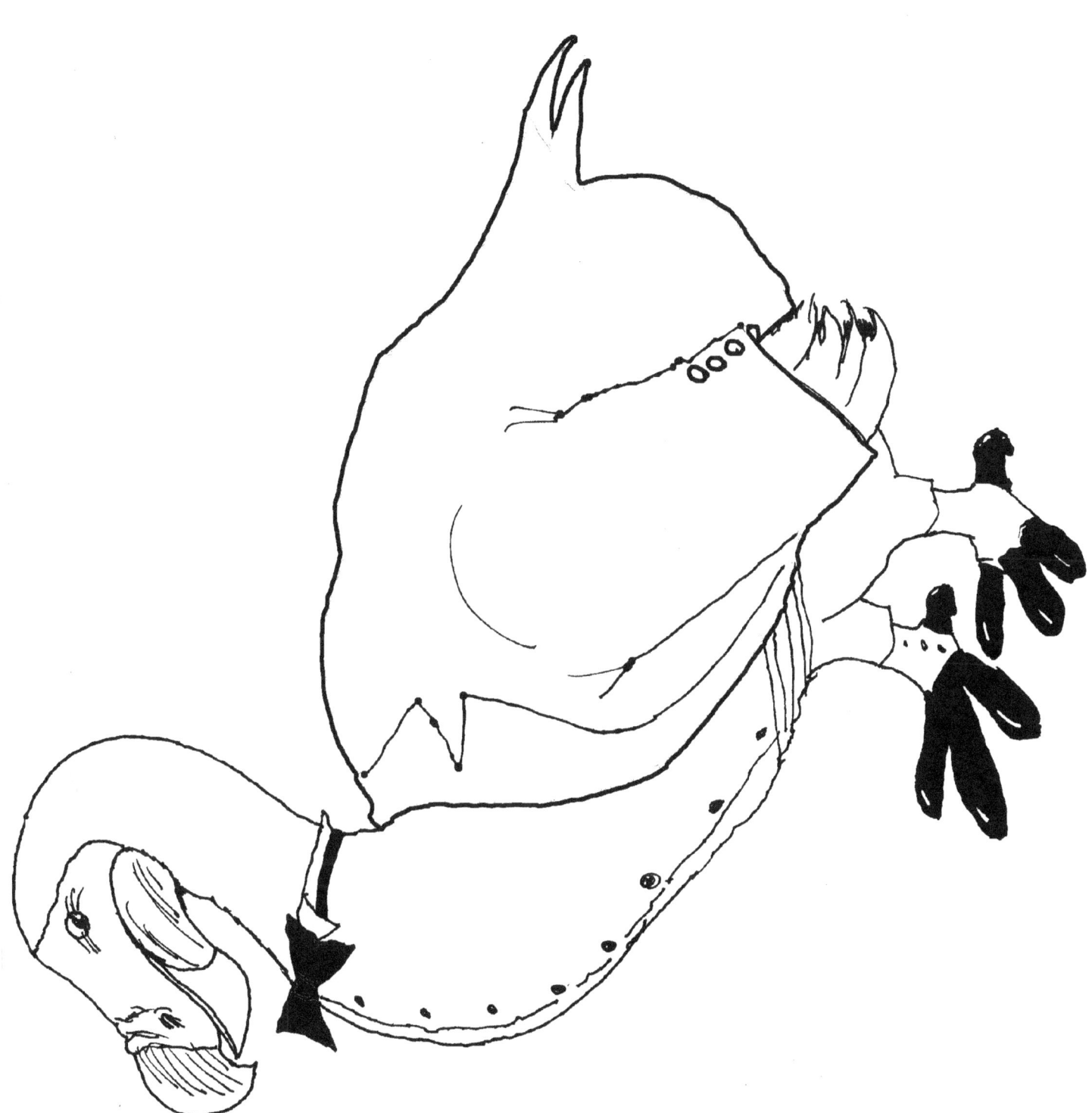

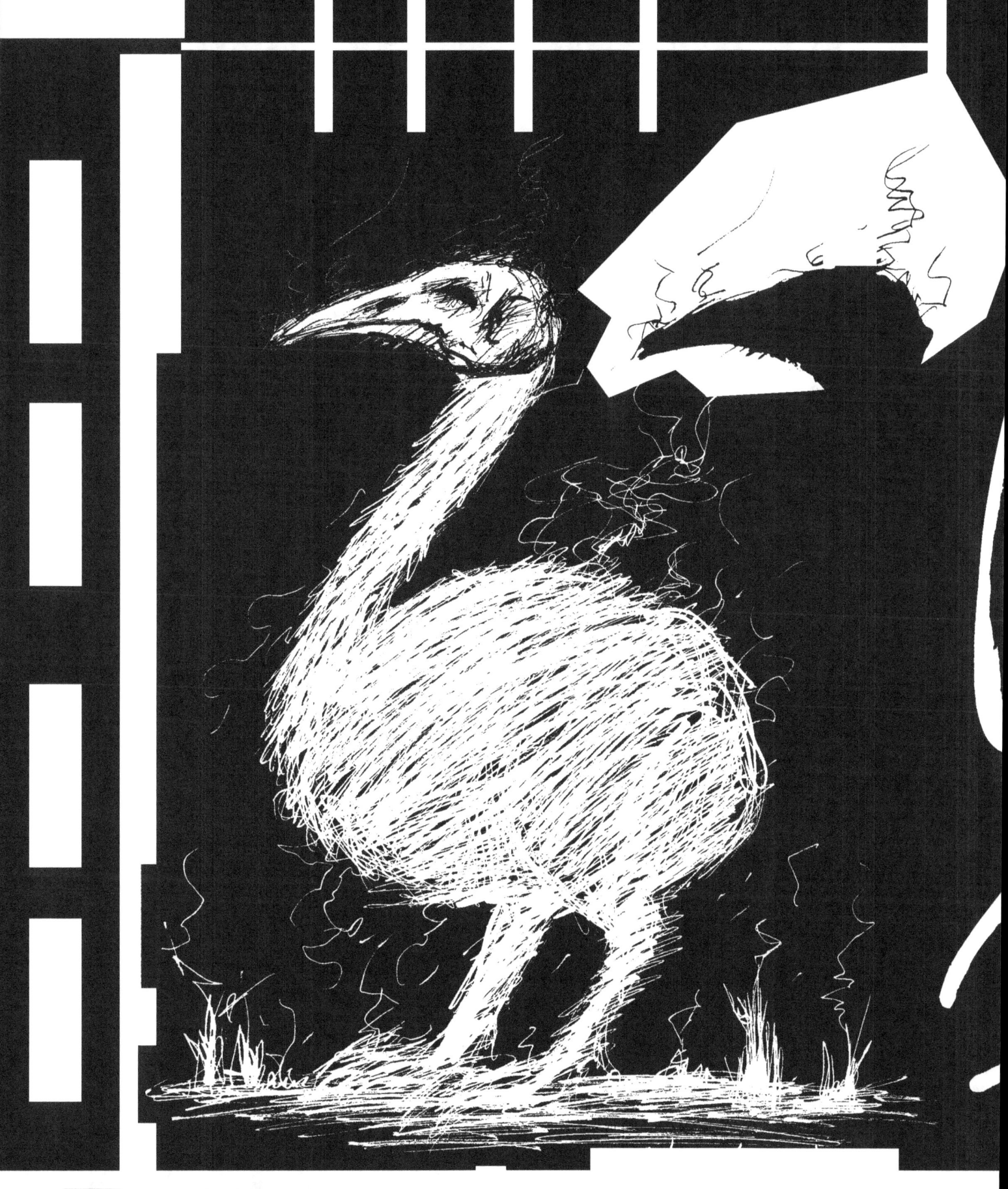

ARTIST'S TIP: This is another one where you could use a translucent coloring method rather than an opaque one.

24

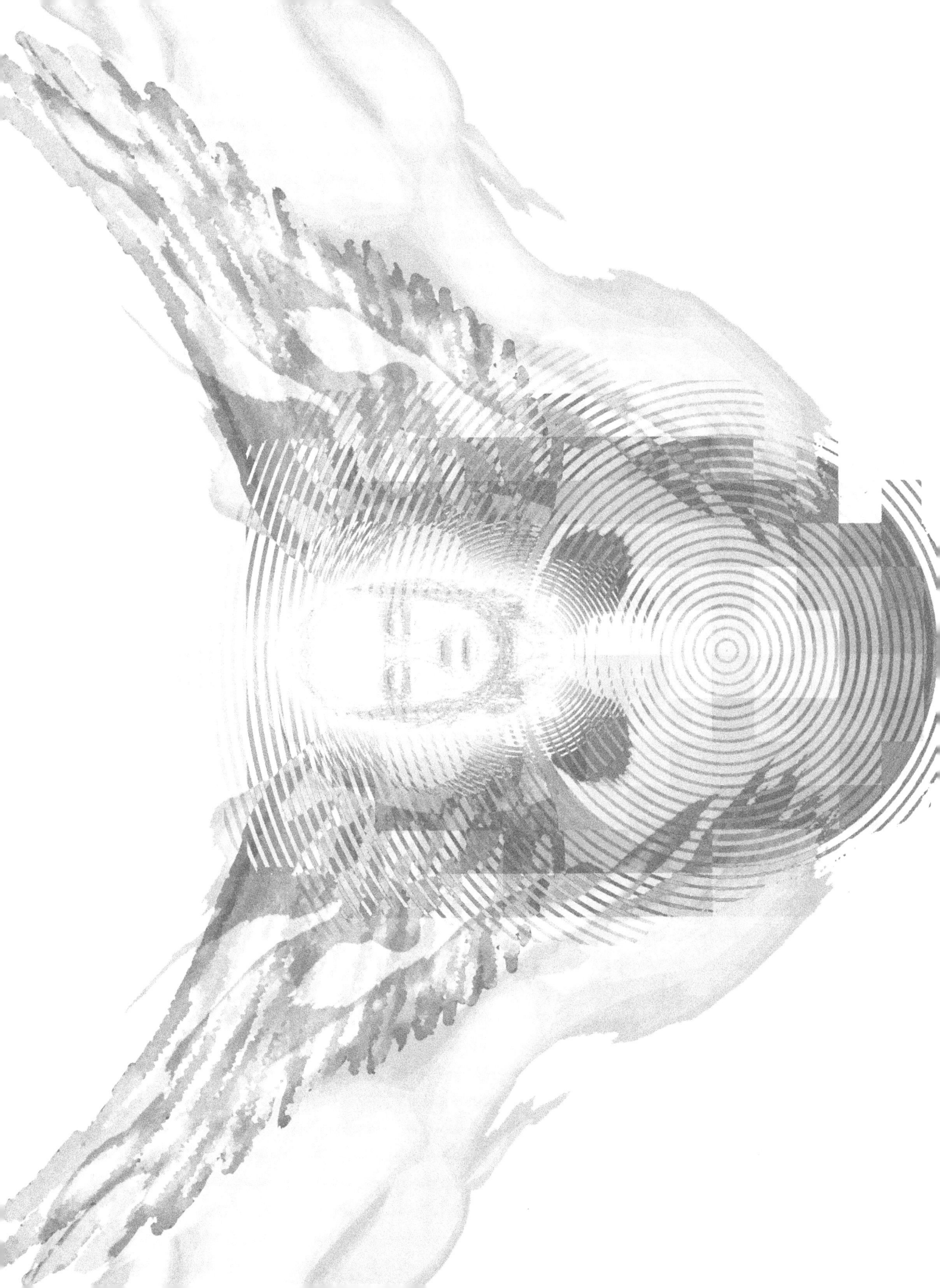

ARTIST'S TIP: A good color palette might be blue for the car, yellow or yellow gold for the statue and skull, and violet or green for the background that is graduated in value from bottom, with the top being the lightest tint.

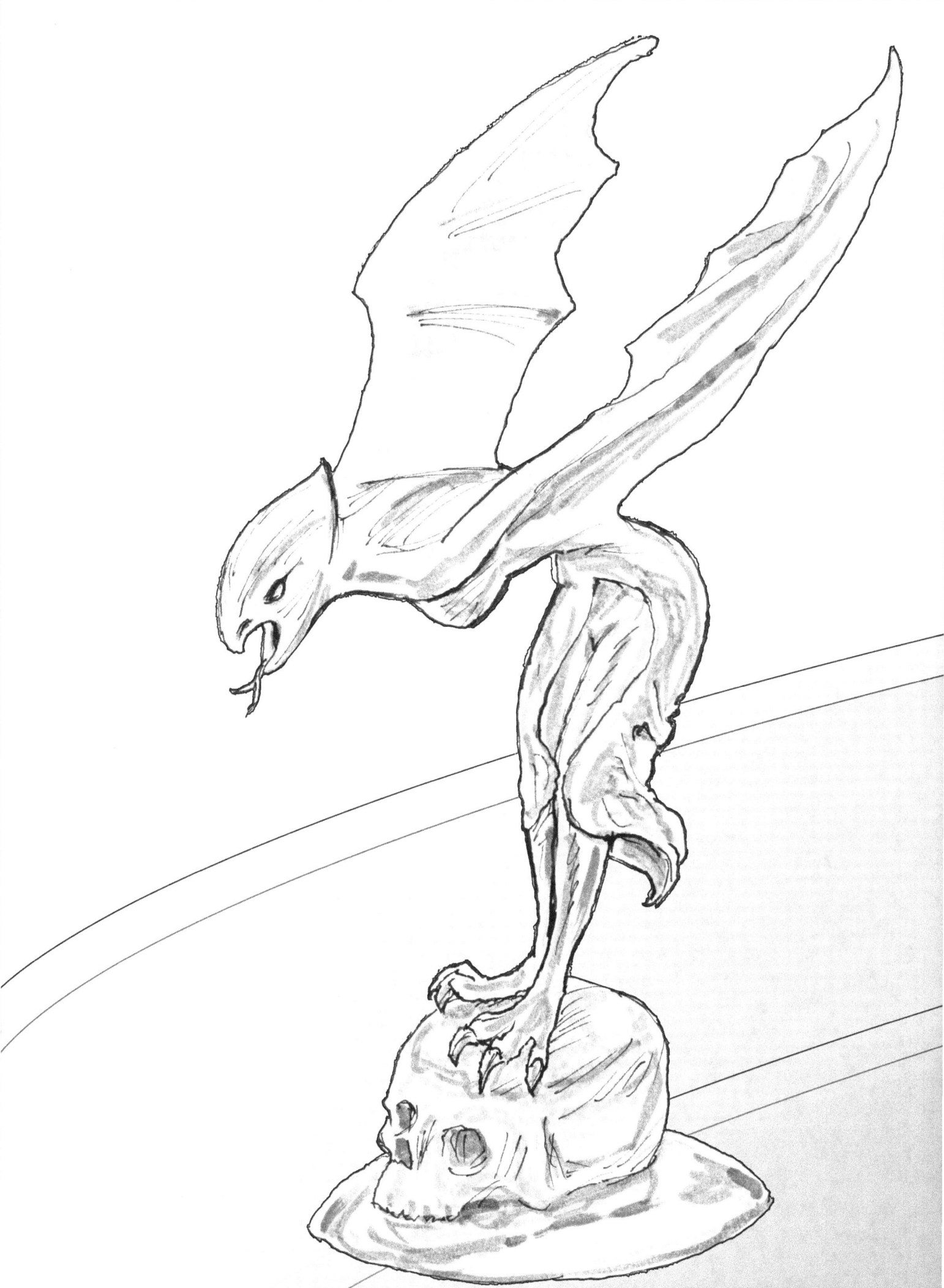

ARTIST'S TIP: Try mixing media on this one. Use markers on the darker values and opaque colors where there are large areas of the white of the paper,

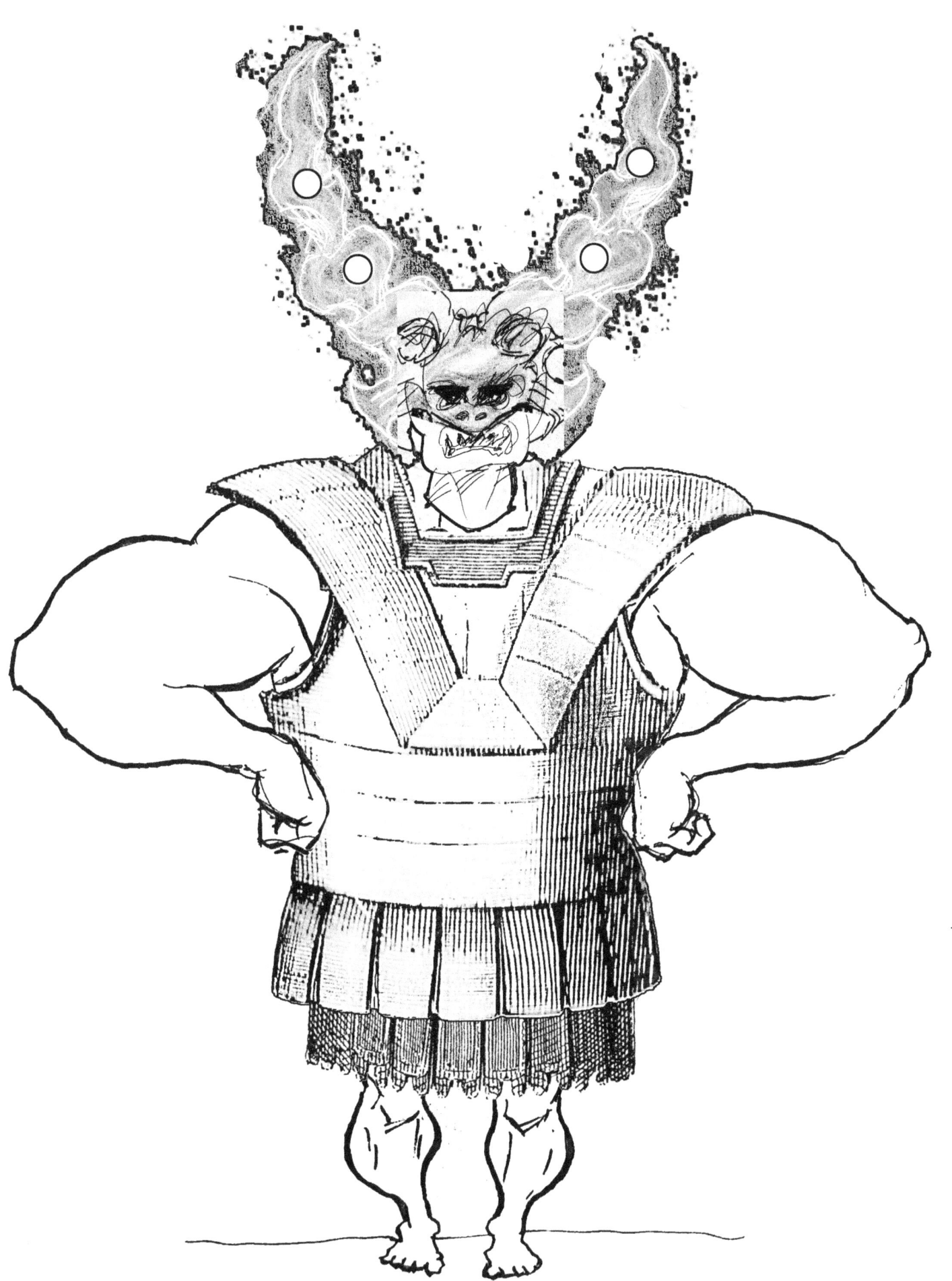

ARTIST'S TIP: This one might be challenging for those who like coloring in the background. Perhaps start with the head and torso of the figure so that you can work out the tonality of the skin and the carapace before proceeding to do the background. You could sketch out background ideas on a separate sheet before attempting to complete the printed page. (Note: Even though there are areas with no clear contour edges, if there are specks or marks in those areas (not pure white), then assume these are positive space—part of the foreground and figure— e.g. on the right side of Crab King's torso, where the serratus anterior is, go over the curved edge lightly with pencil, mirroring it with the opposite side of the torso.)

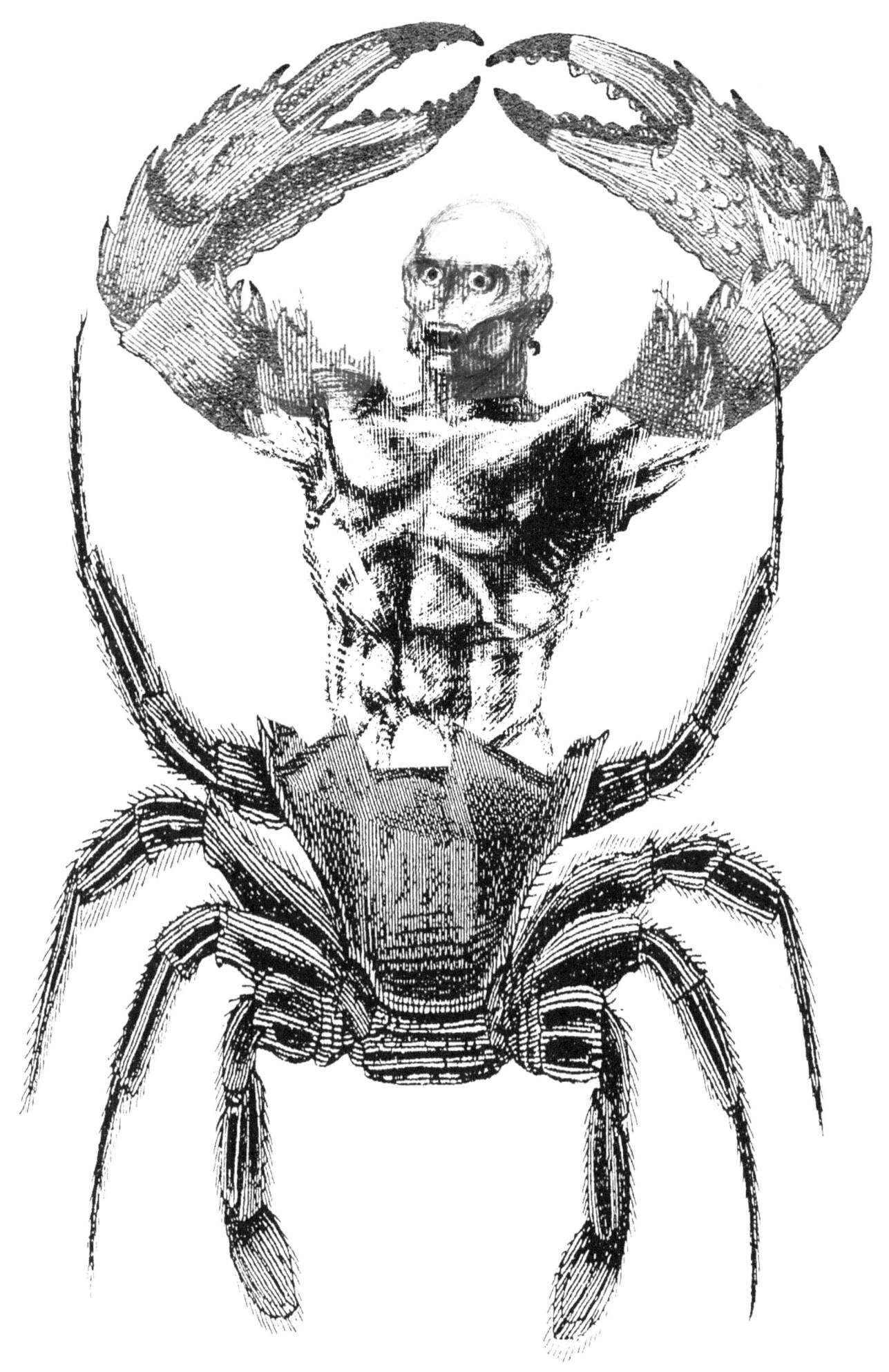

ARTIST'S TIP: Once again, this is an image with a lot of grayscale and little white area. Start with the lightest color markers not darker ones—begin with the head and torso and work your way out so that you can have a good idea of your subject and how to integrate it with the background color scheme.

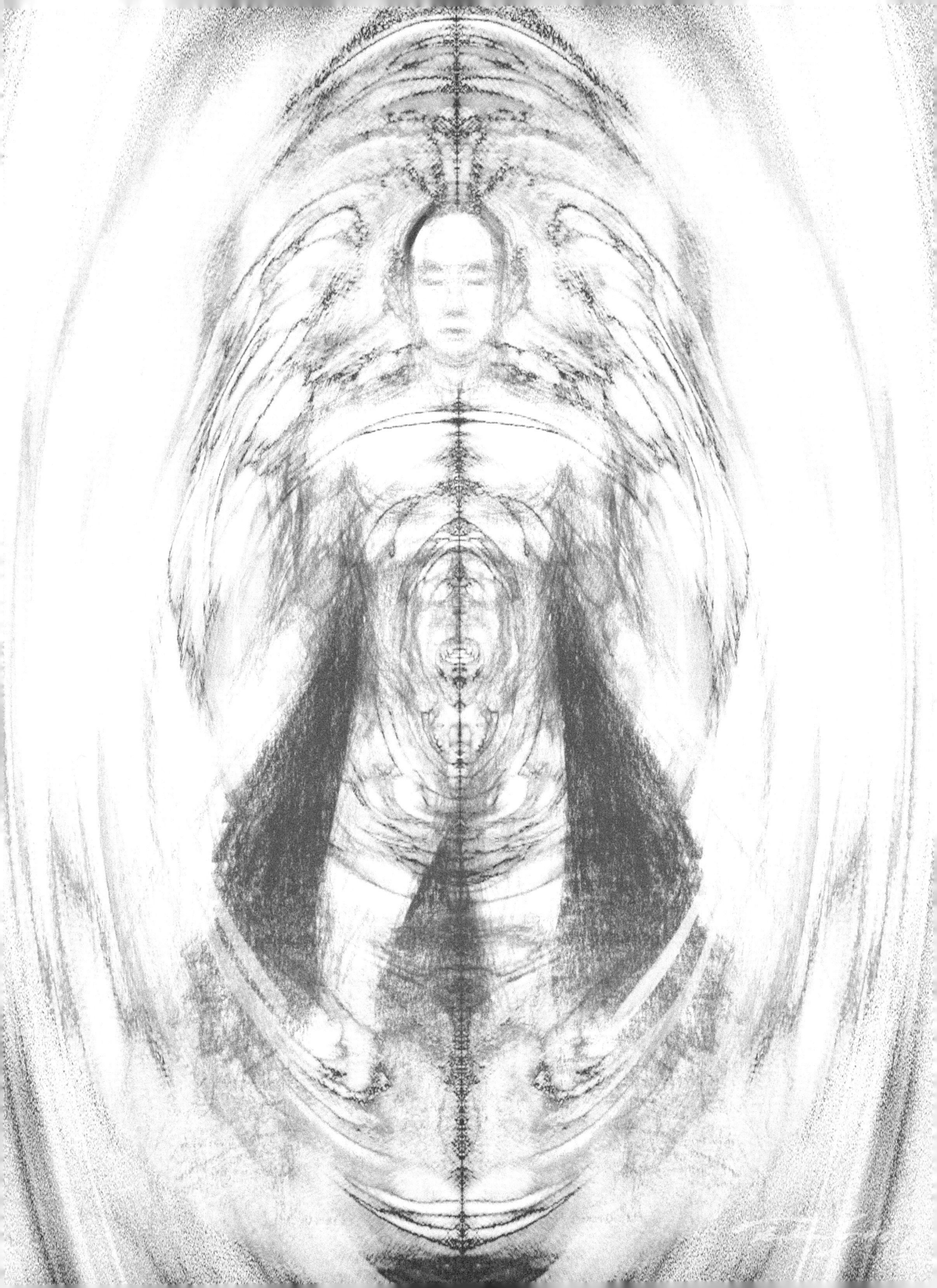

ARTIST'S TIP: Just enjoy coloring this one!

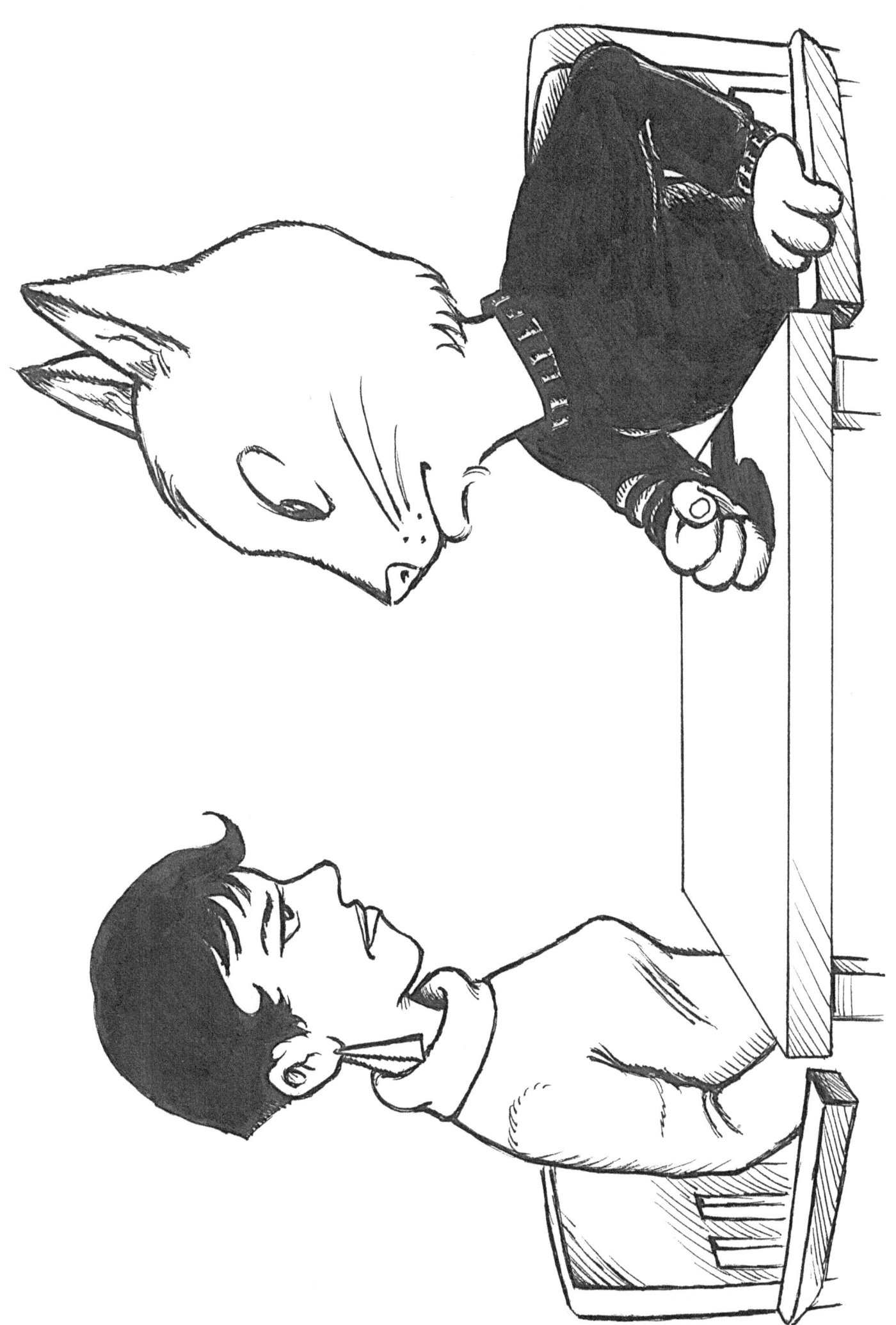

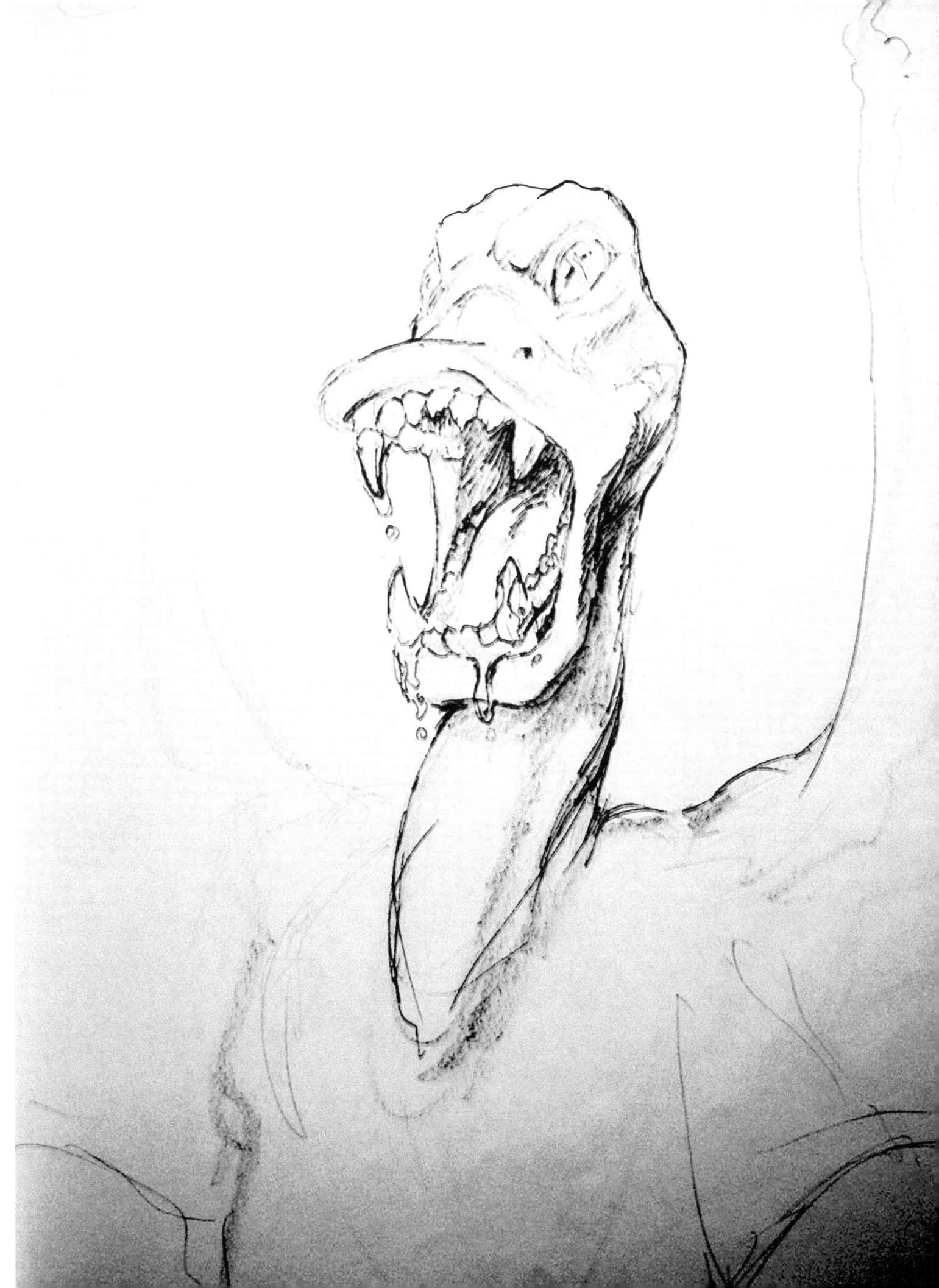

ARTIST'S TIP: This might be a fun opportunity to try crayon resist (lay down crayon strokes first then color in with a translucent marker. Again, you may make copies to practice on before completing the printed image.

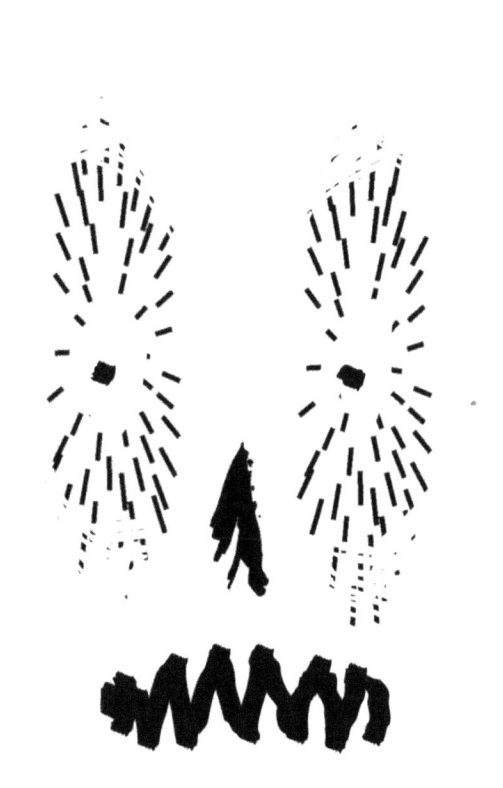

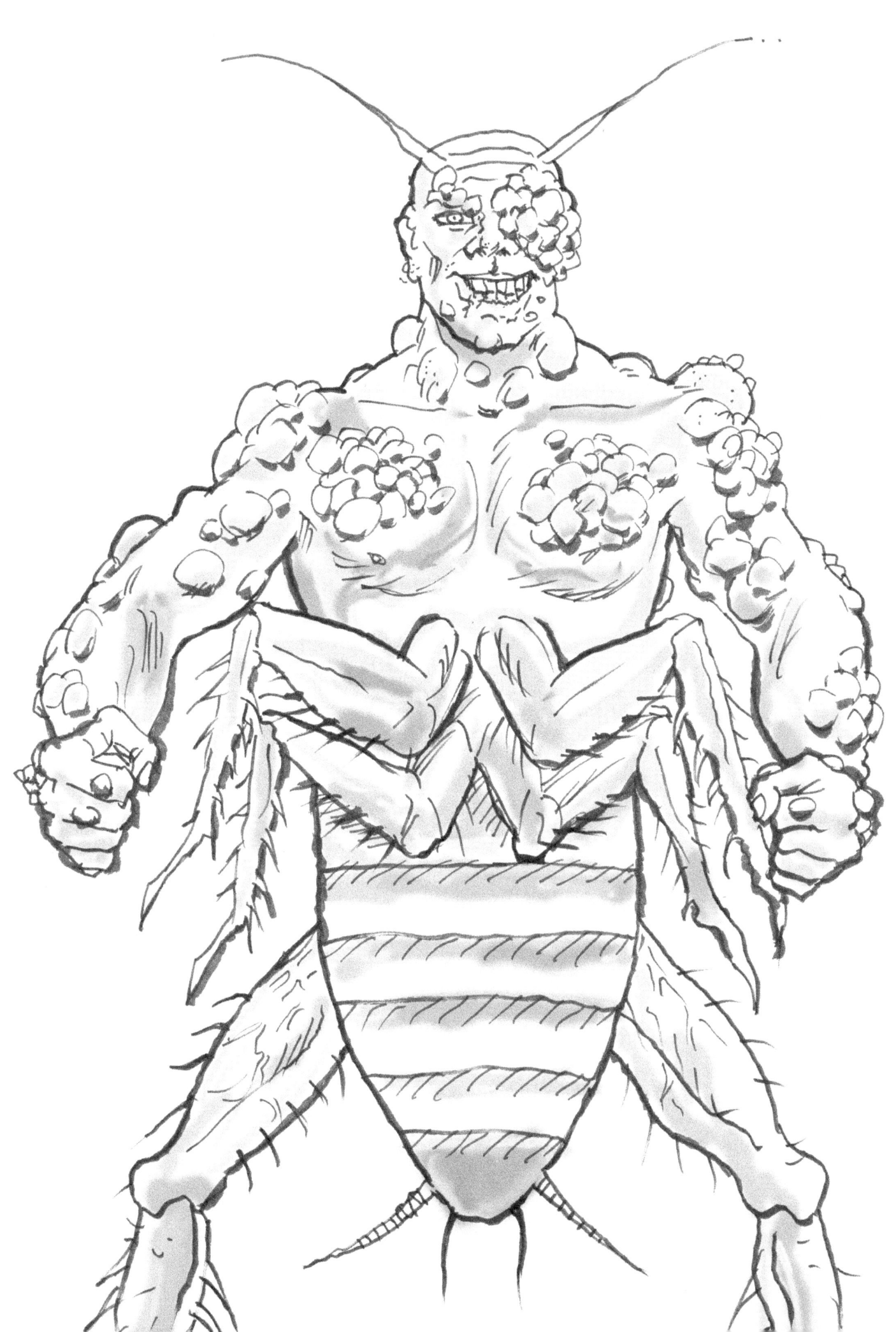

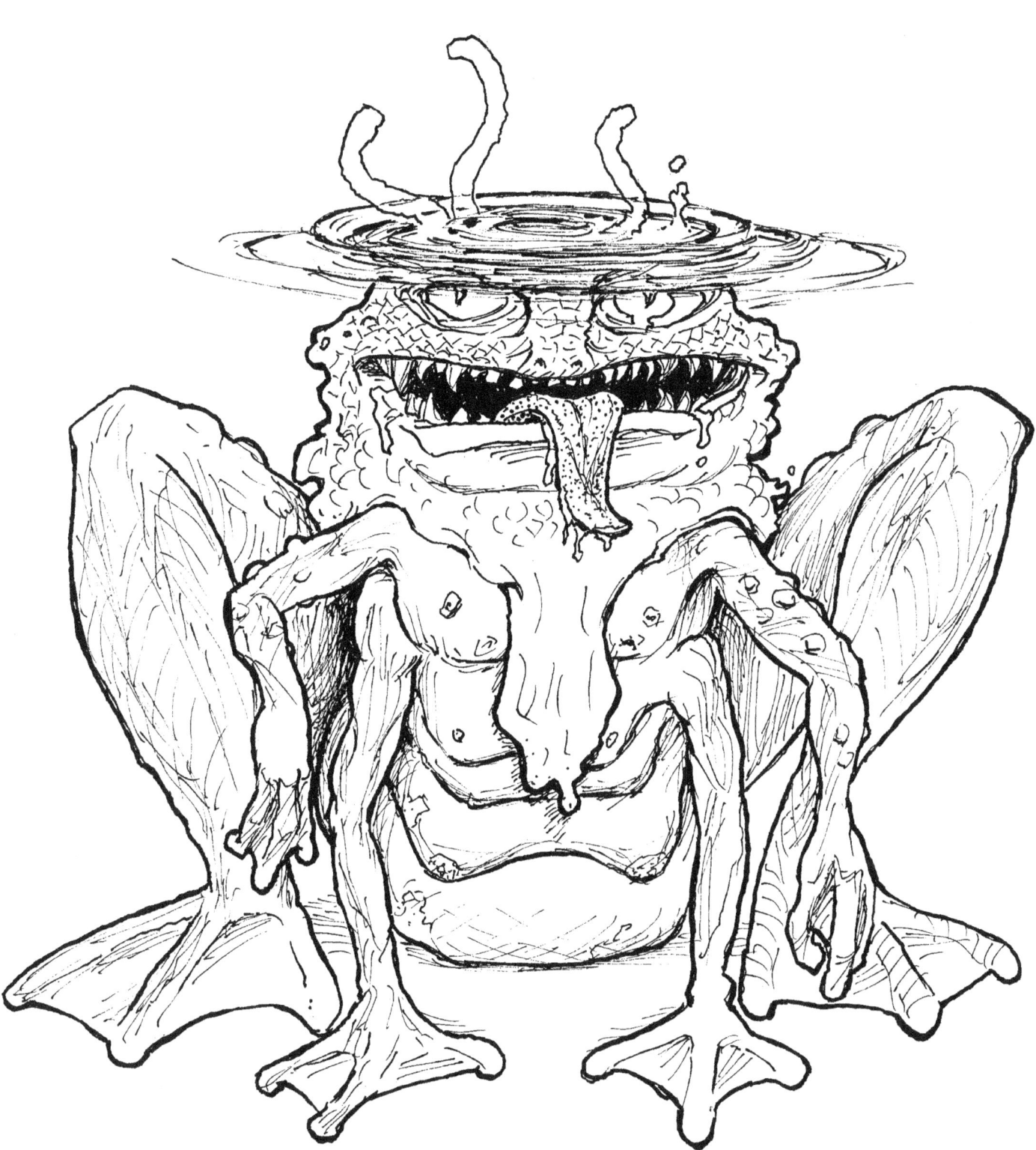

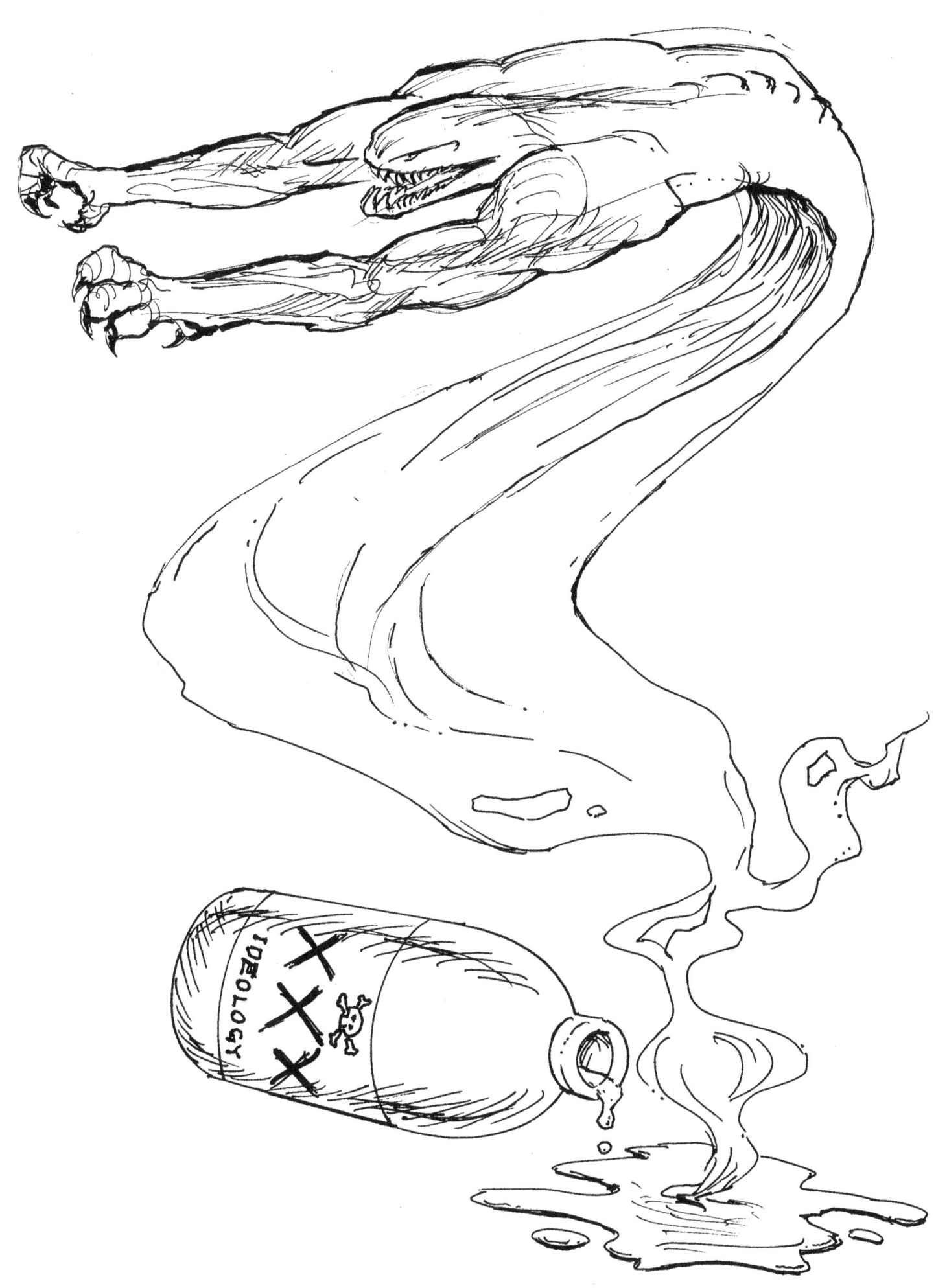

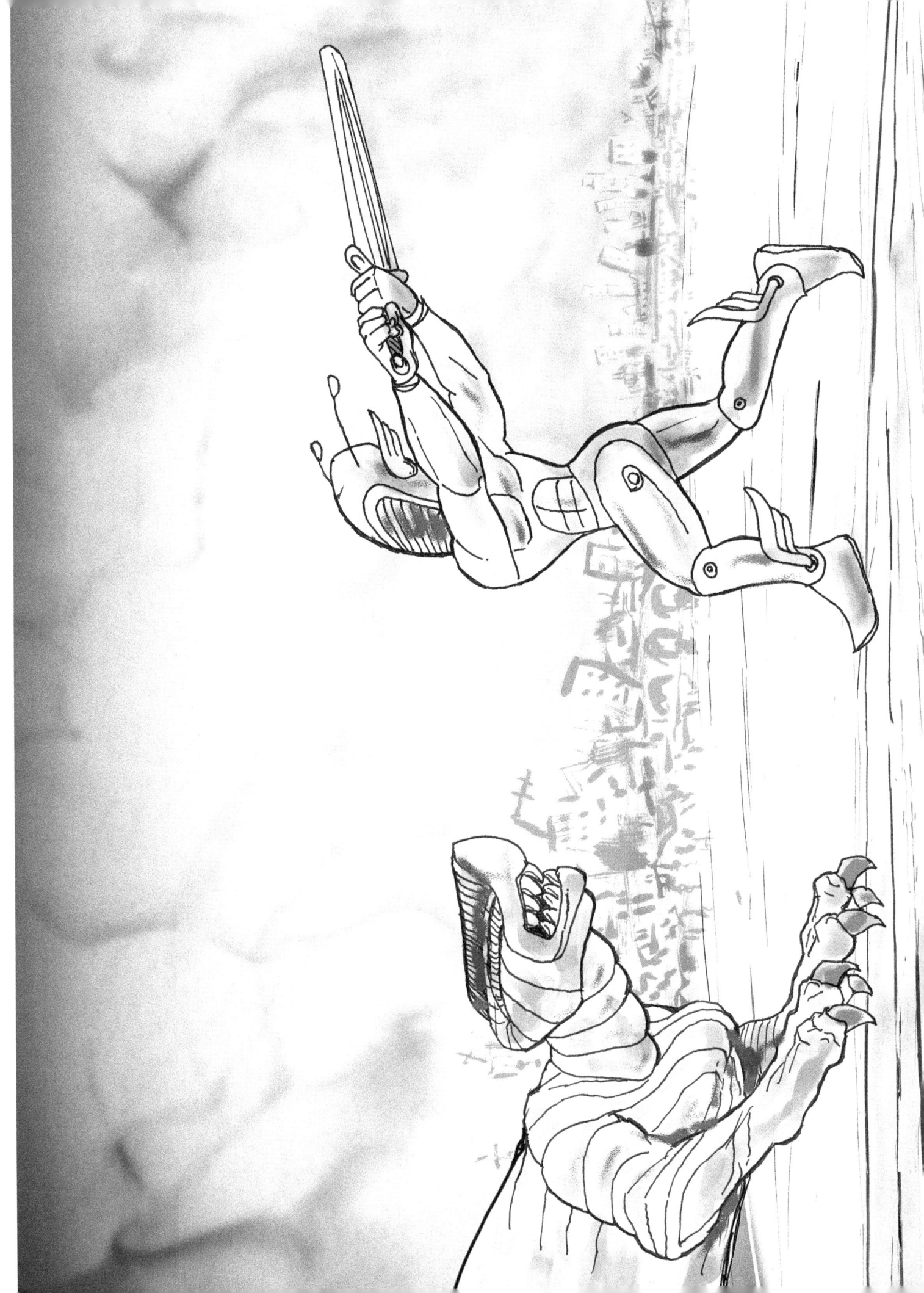

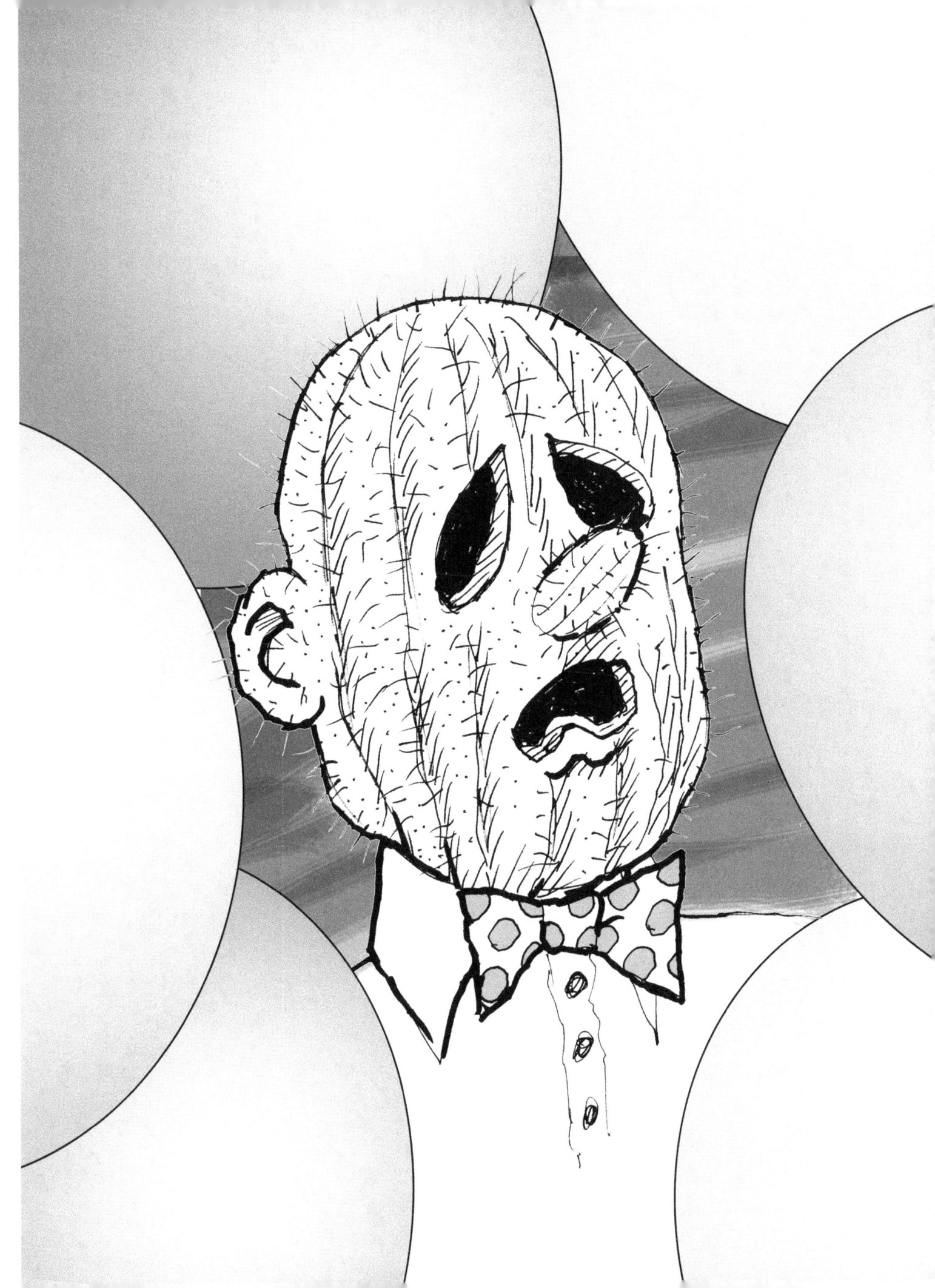

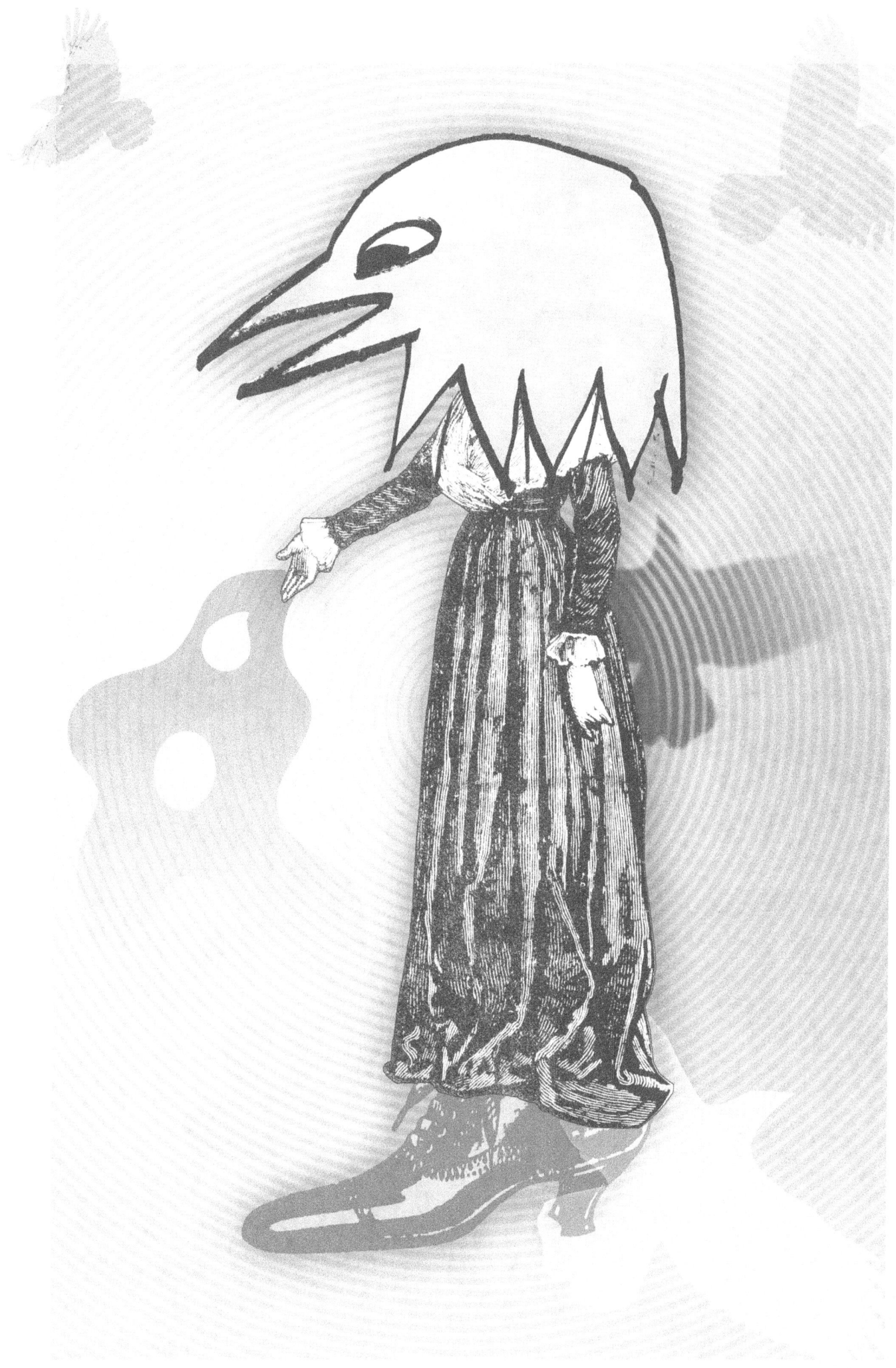

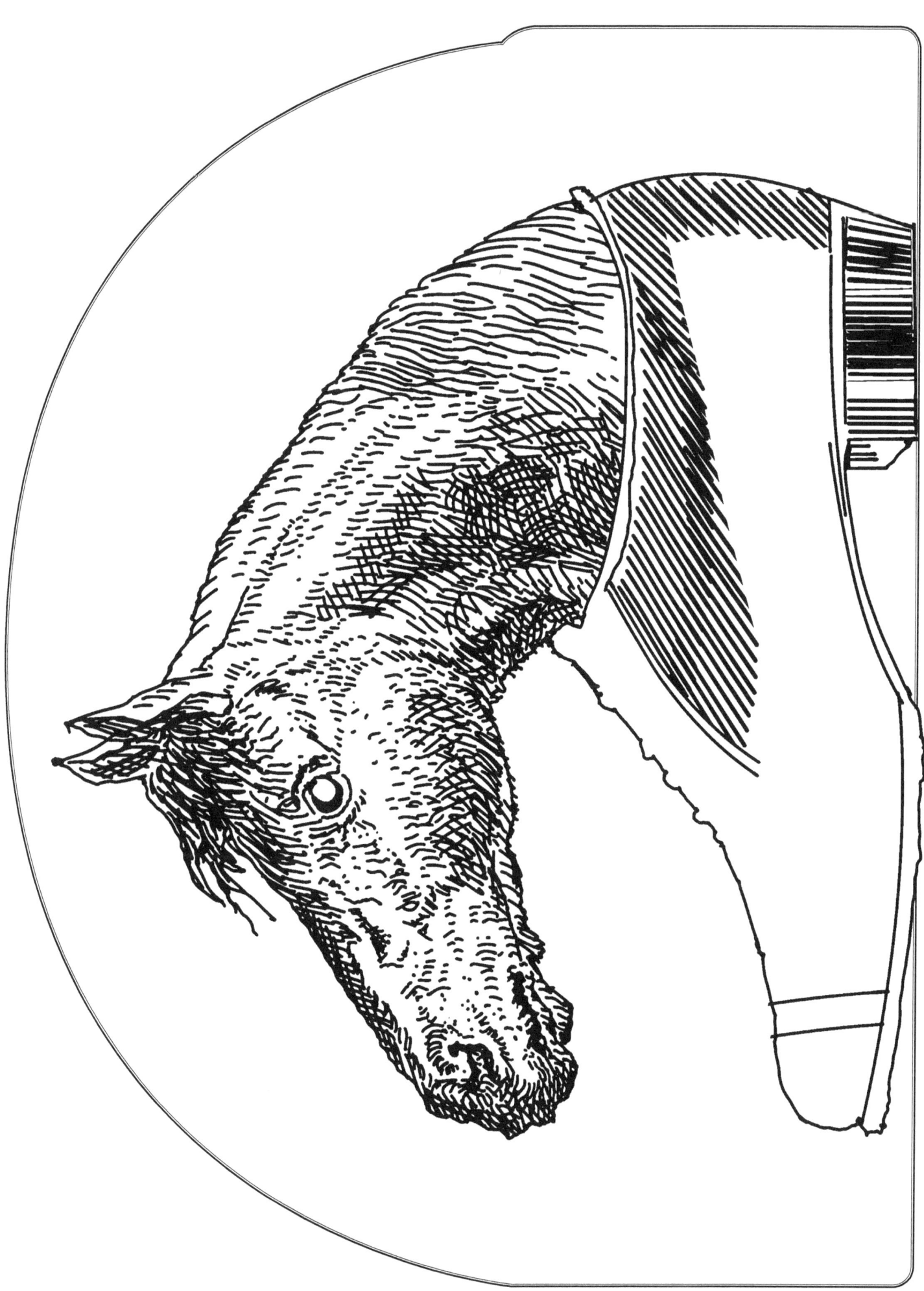

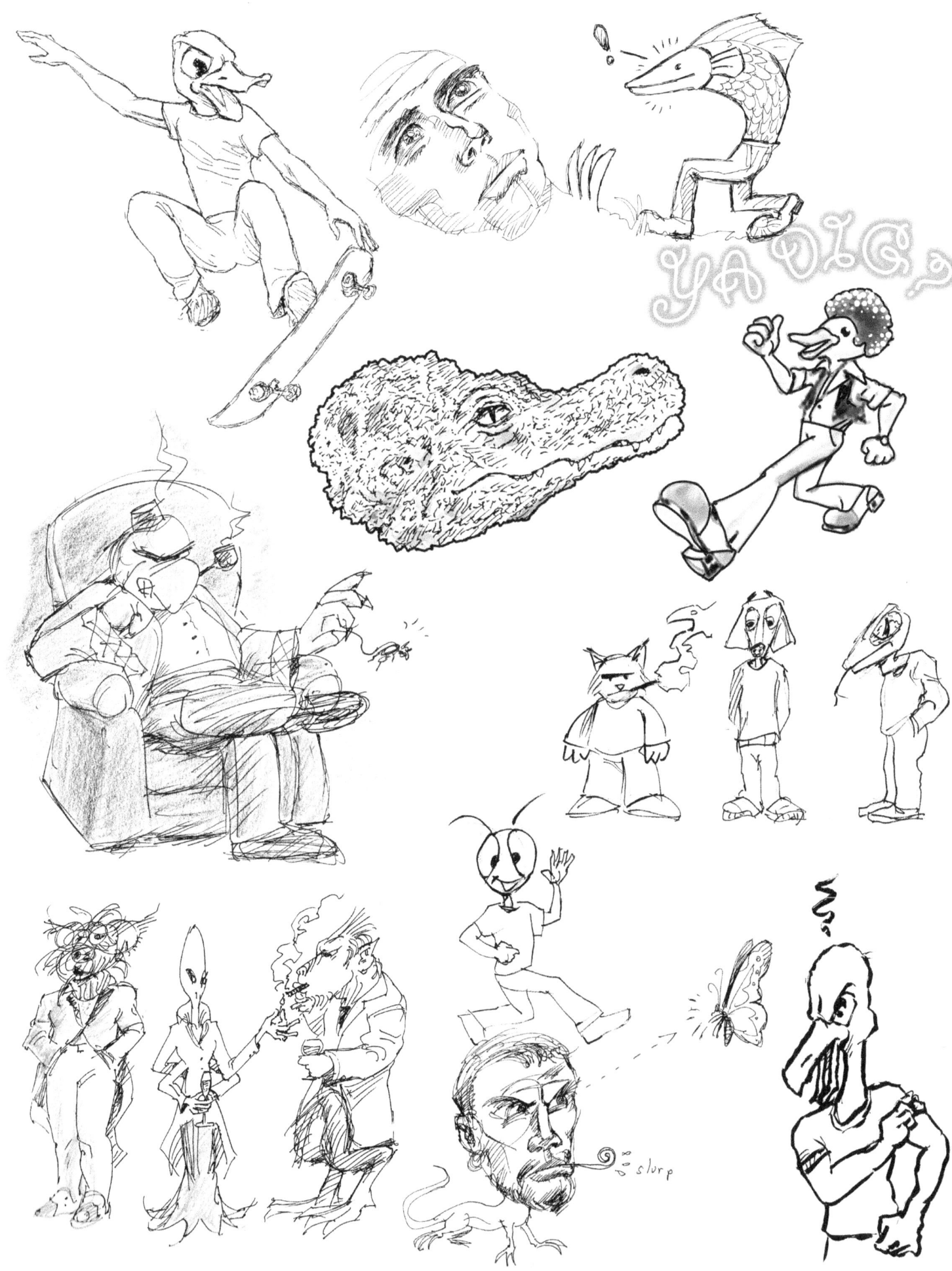

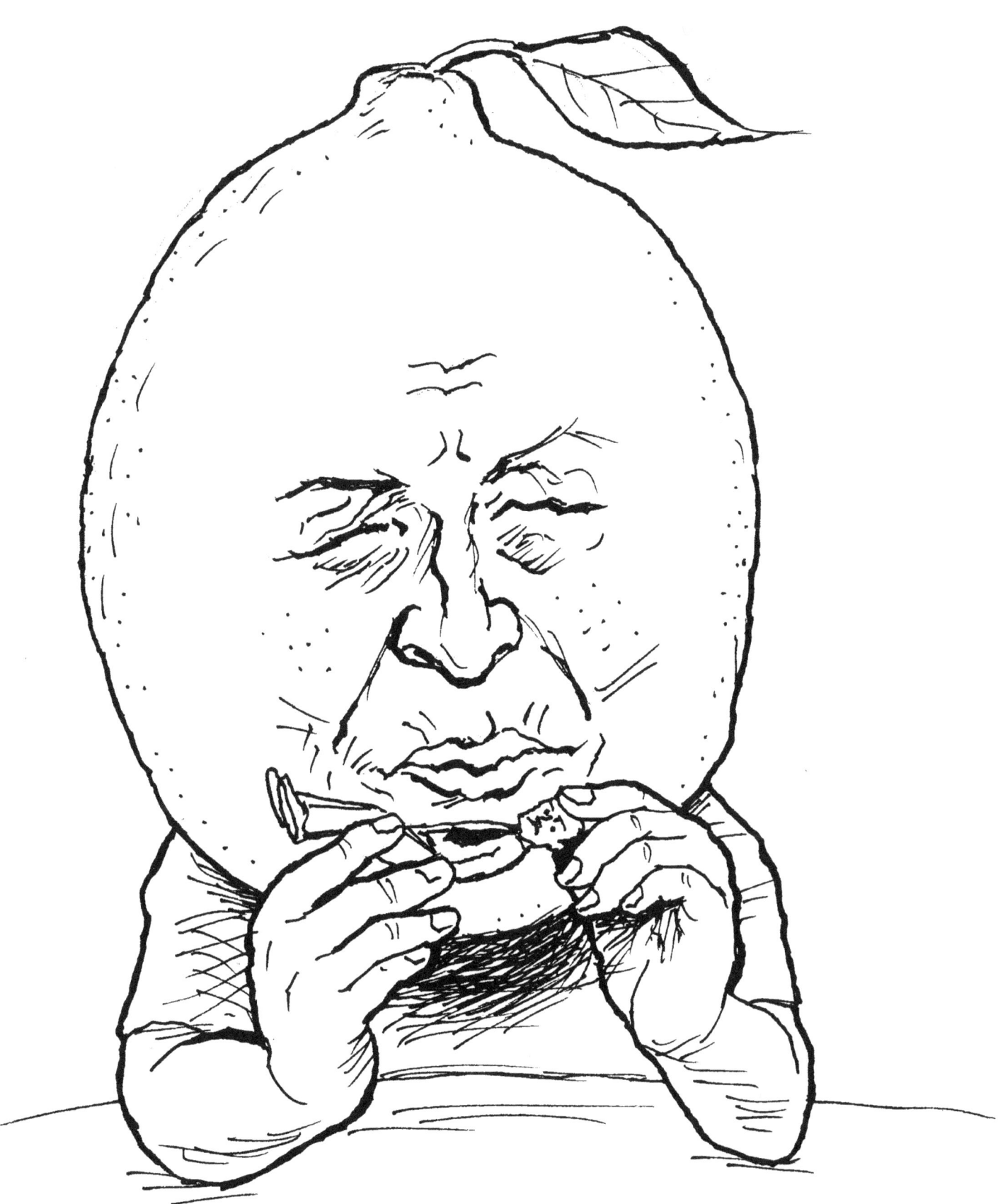

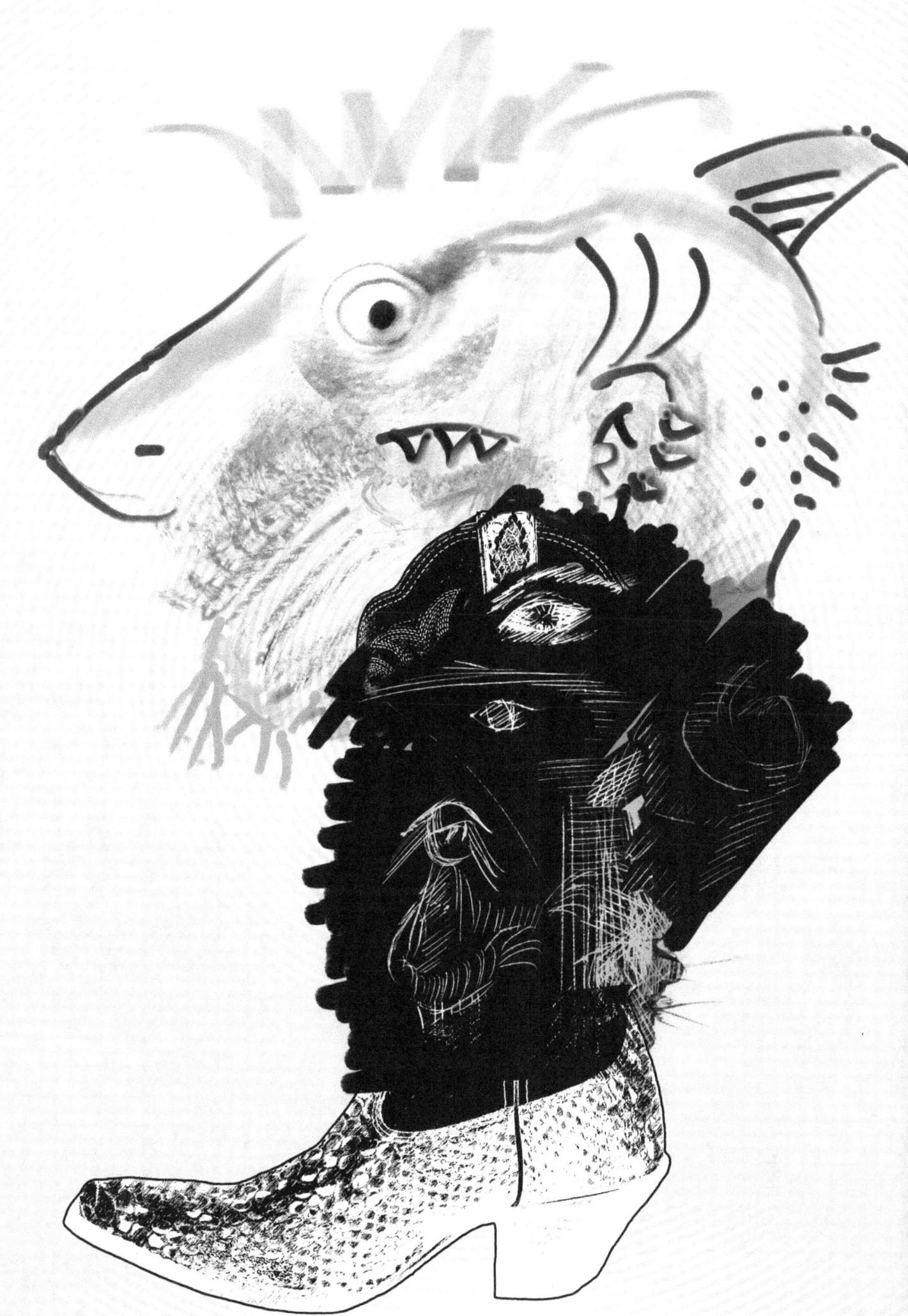

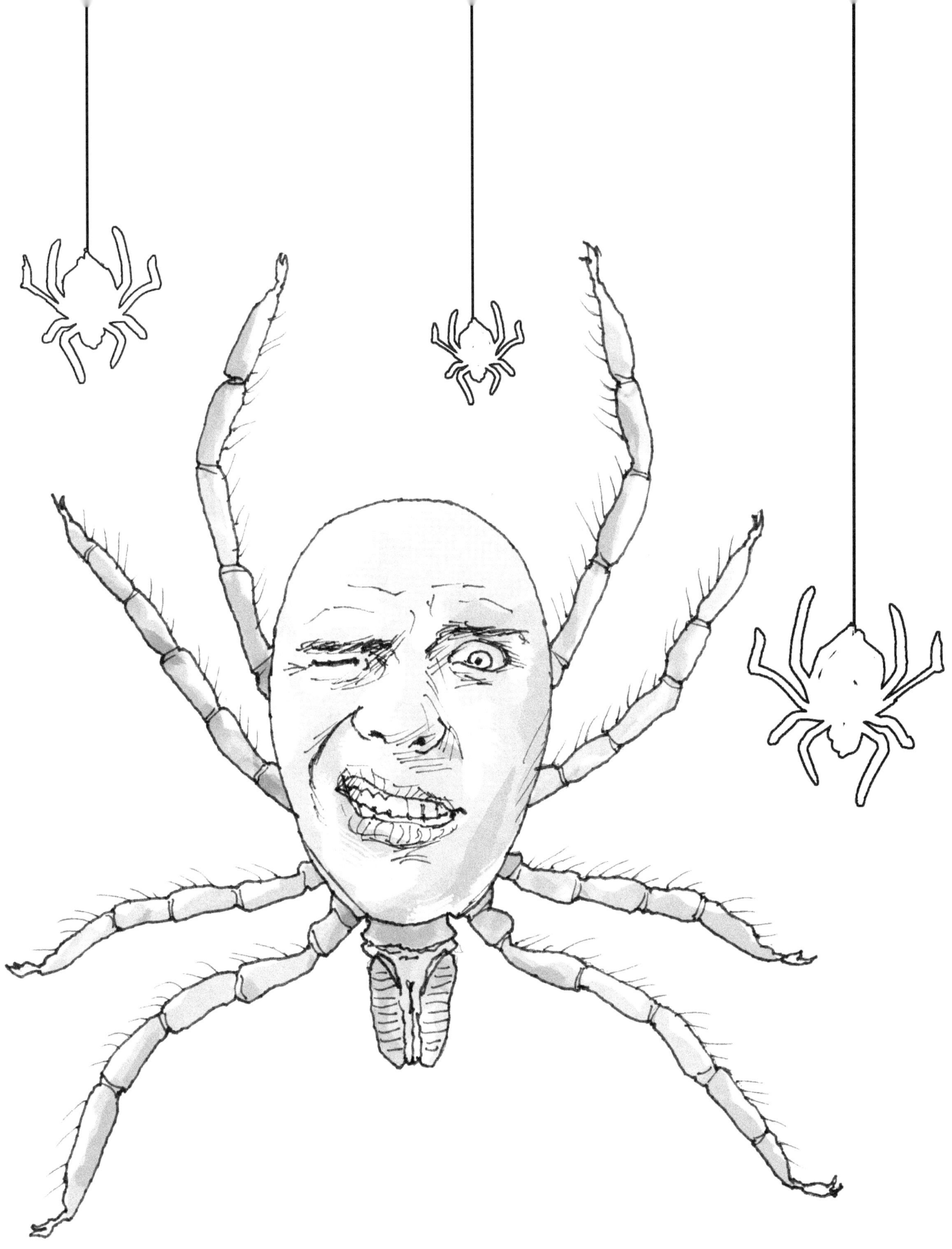

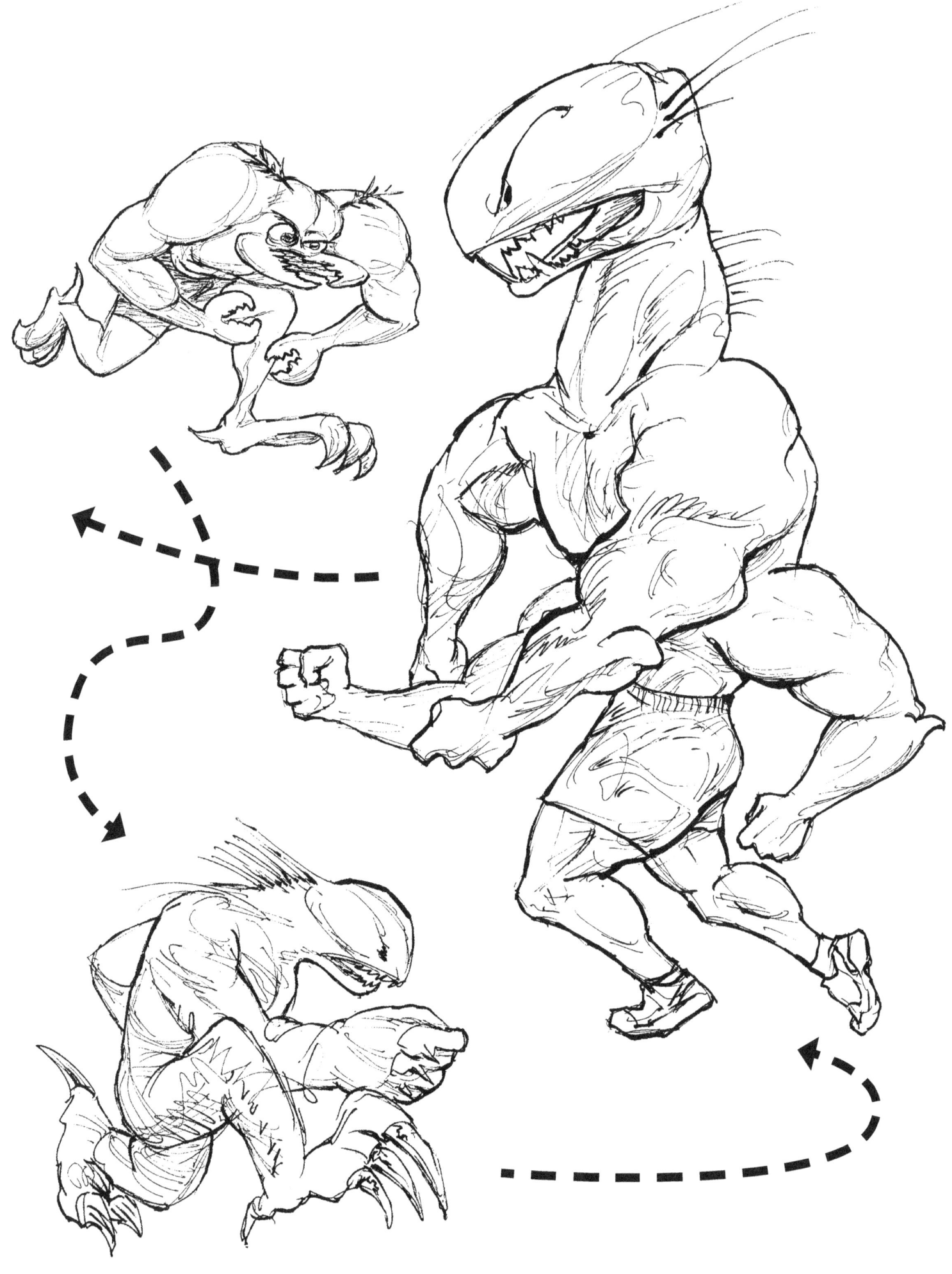

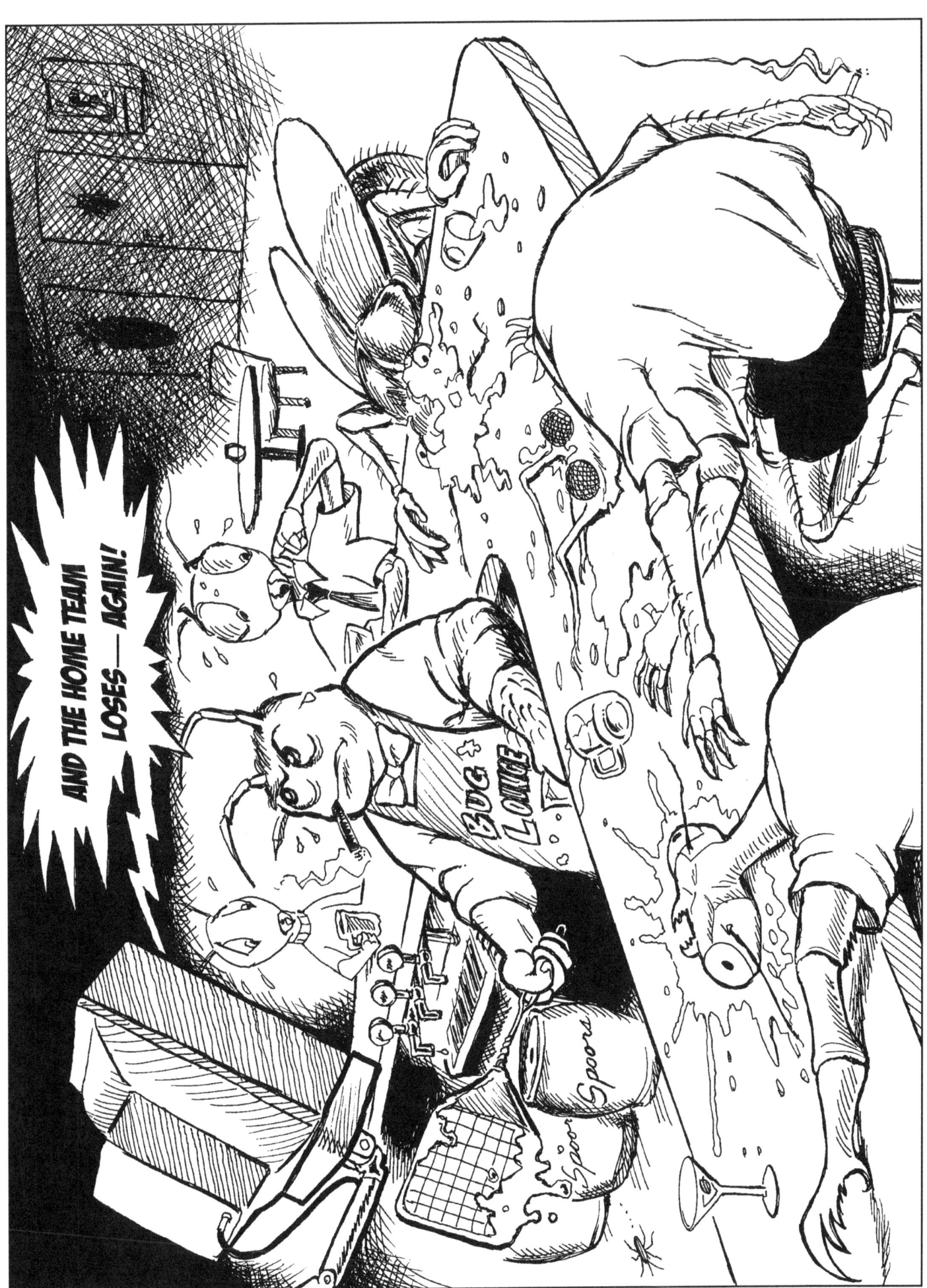

ARTIST'S TIP: Have plenty of loose change in the car. Seriously though, this image would be suitable to any of the recommended media (crayon, pencil, marker), but I'd use translucent marker first on the outer edges of the raccoon where there are detailed strokes of the animal's fur. Then find a matching tone using color pencil and start in light but build it up as you work further into the center areas.

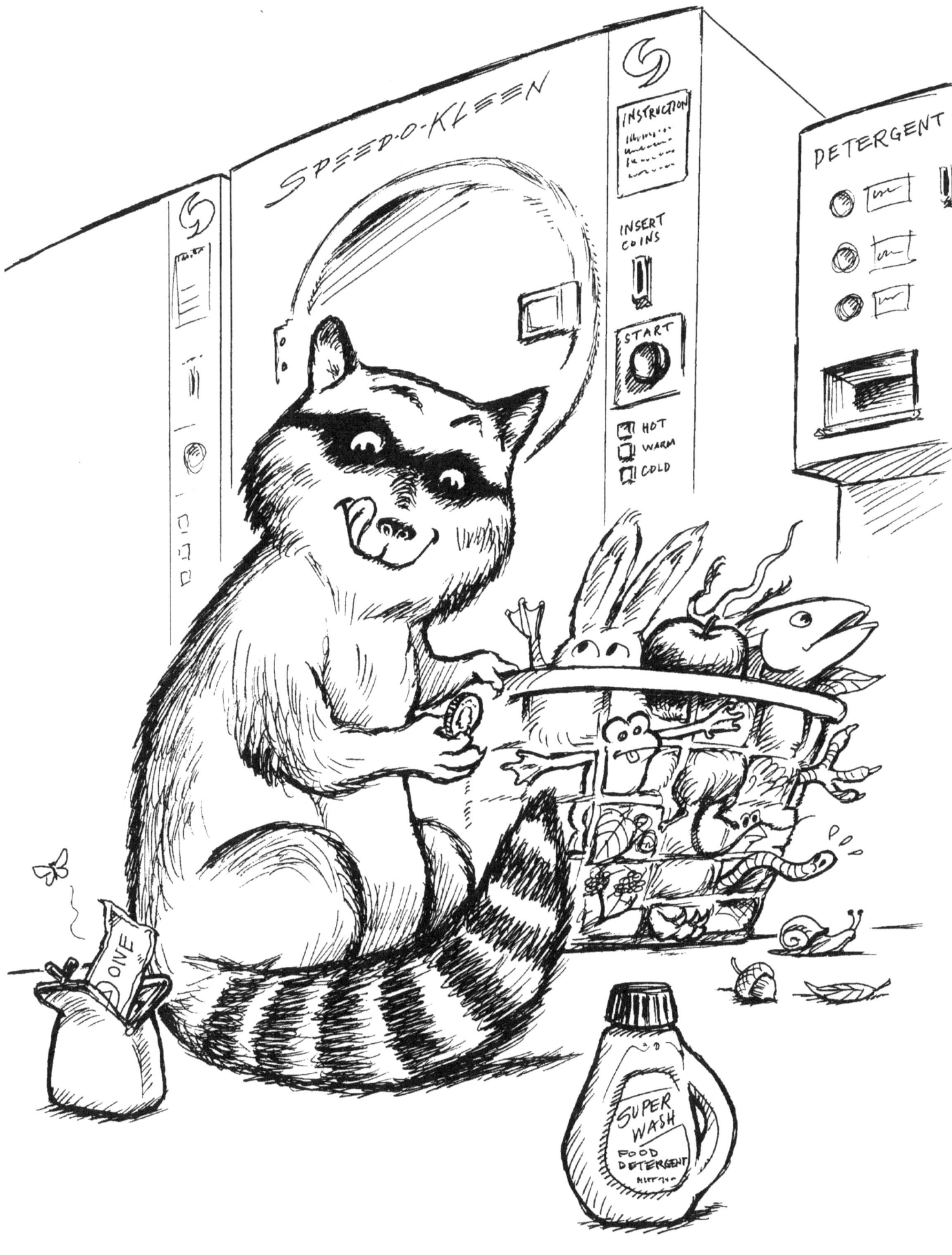

ARTIST'S TIP: Highlighter markers would be great for the interior of the medallion surrounding Death Dog's head and maybe a deep red tone for the background? Just a suggestion.

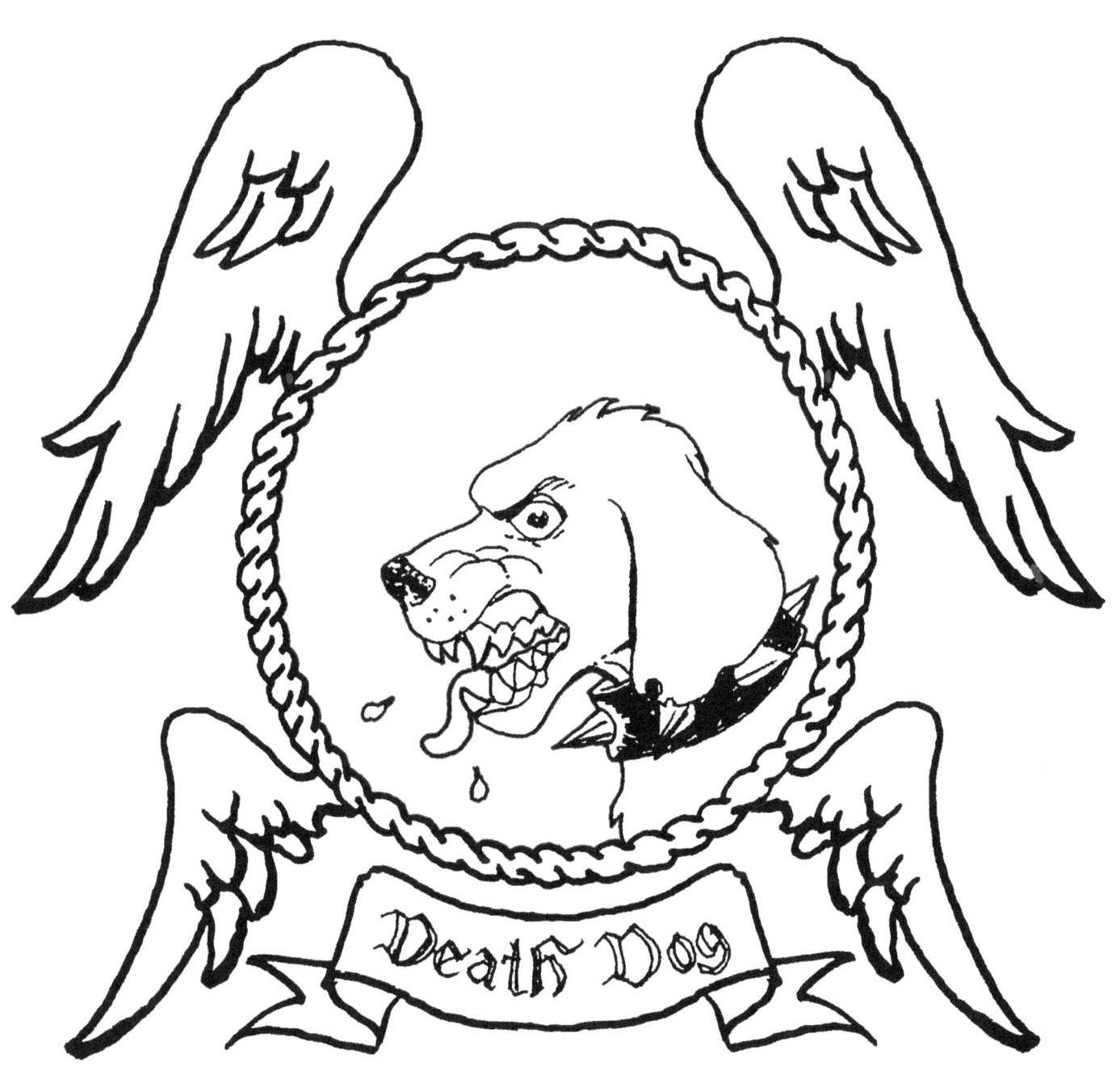

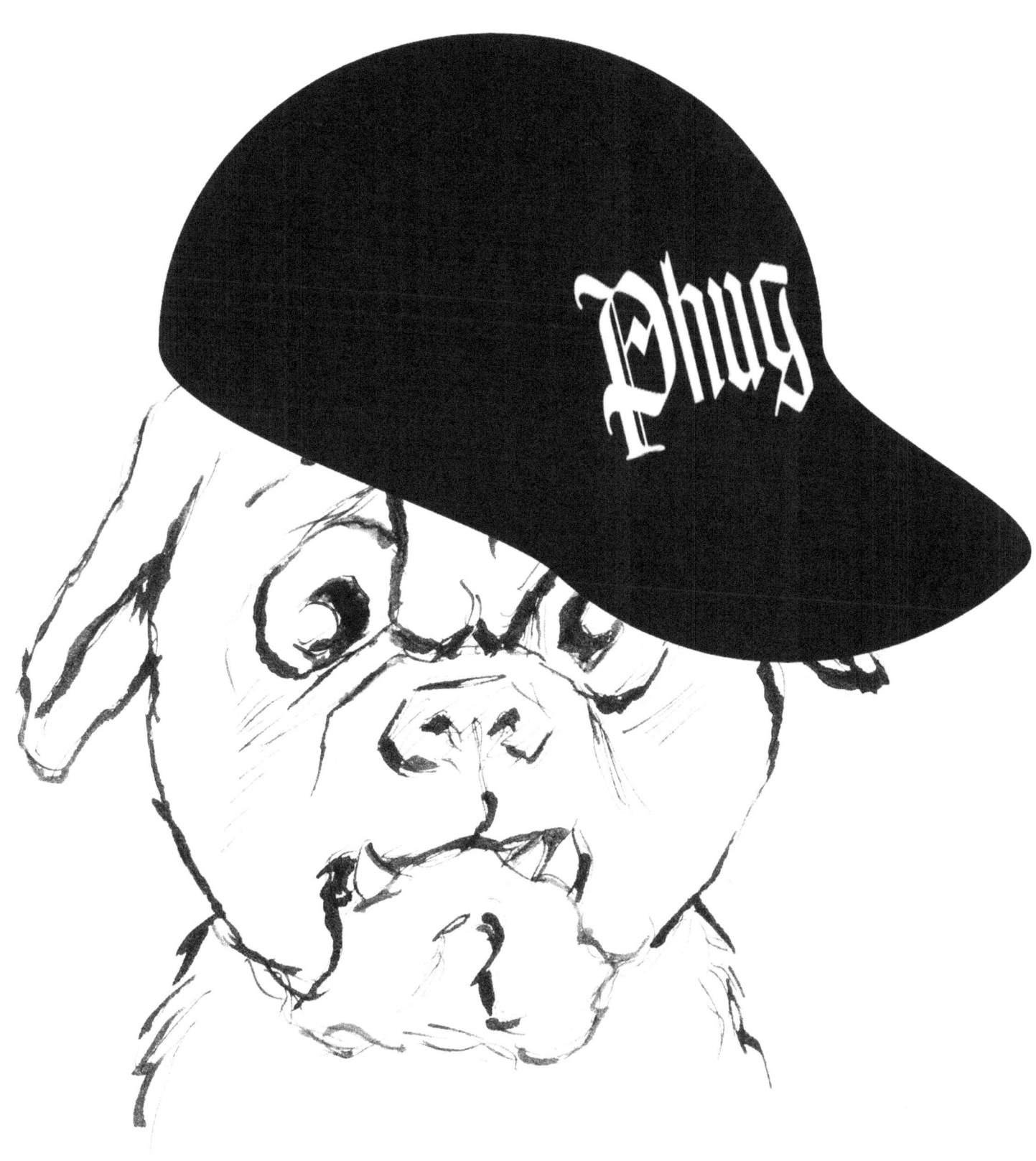

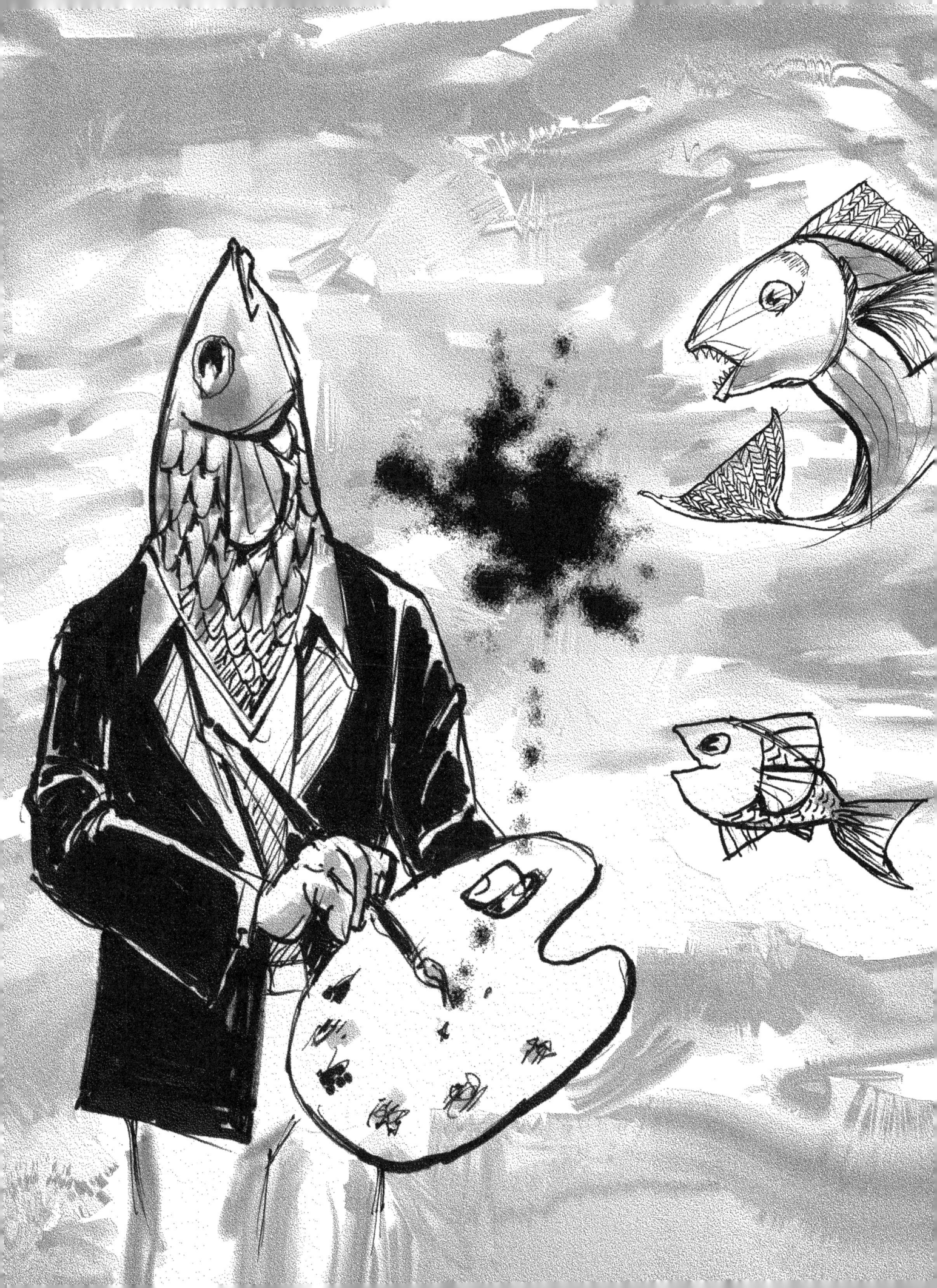

ARTIST'S TIP: Have fun developing a strong color palette for this image.

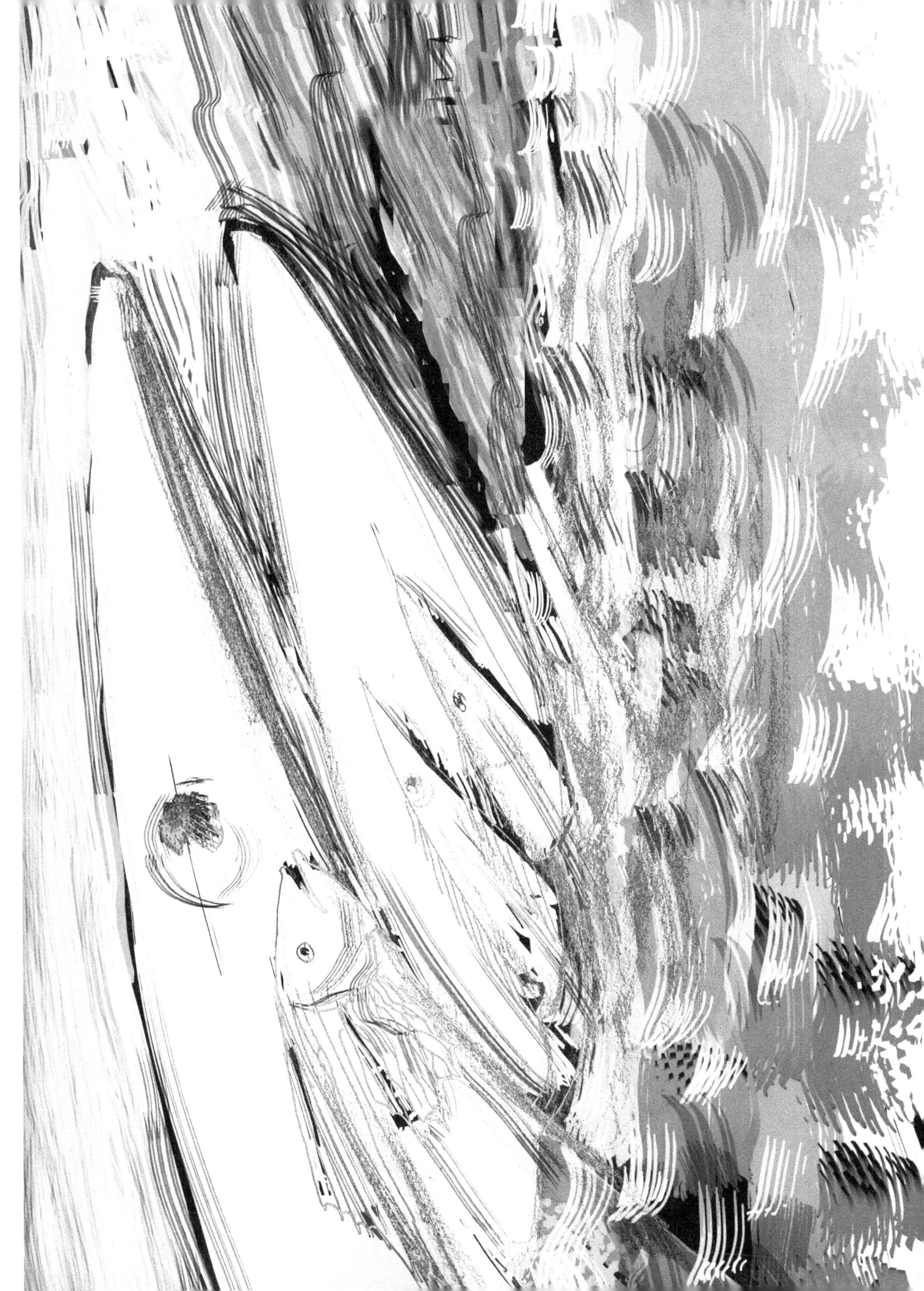

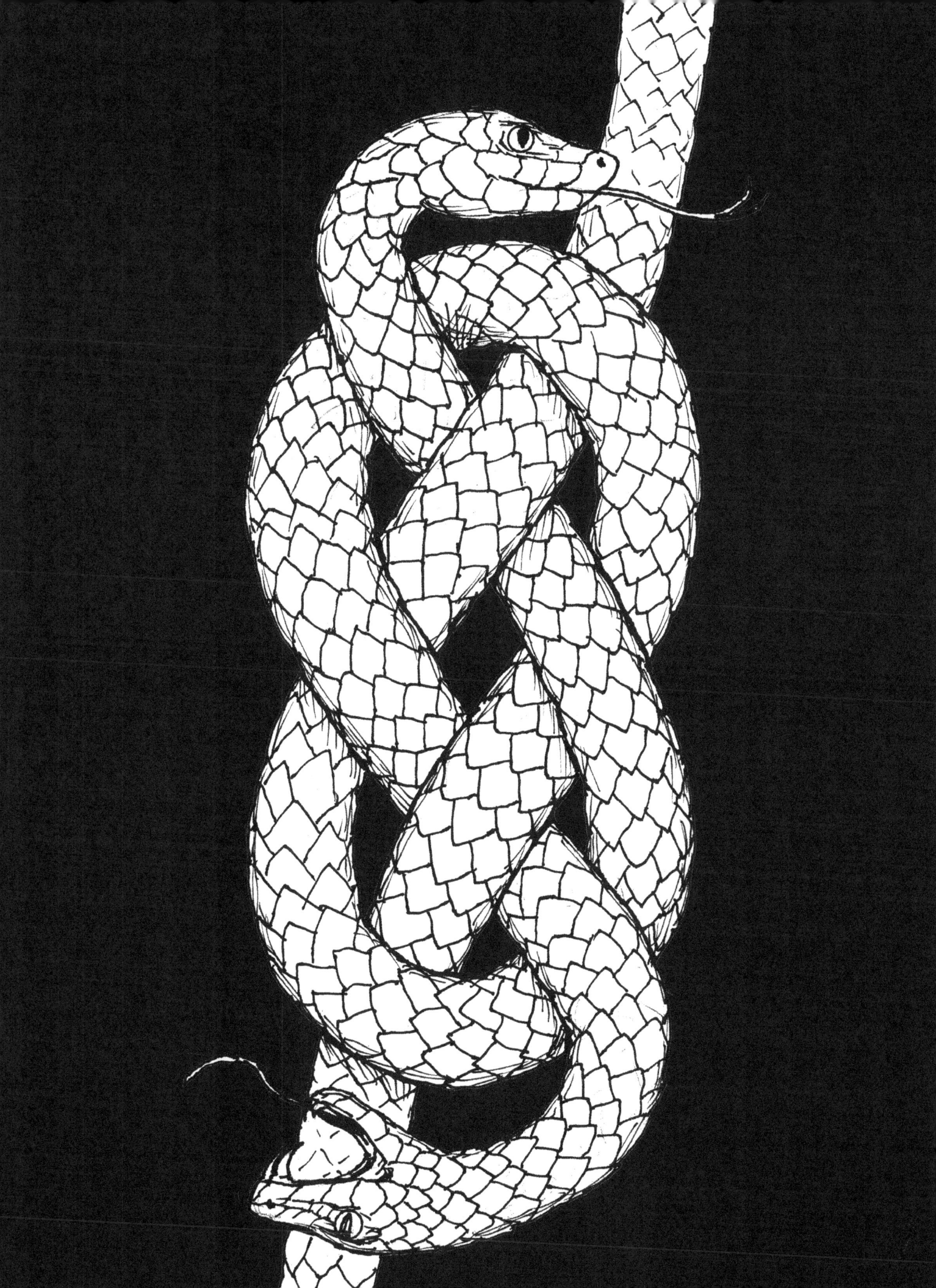

ARTIST'S TIP: This piece has a lot of white space with which to play, so go crazy with it!

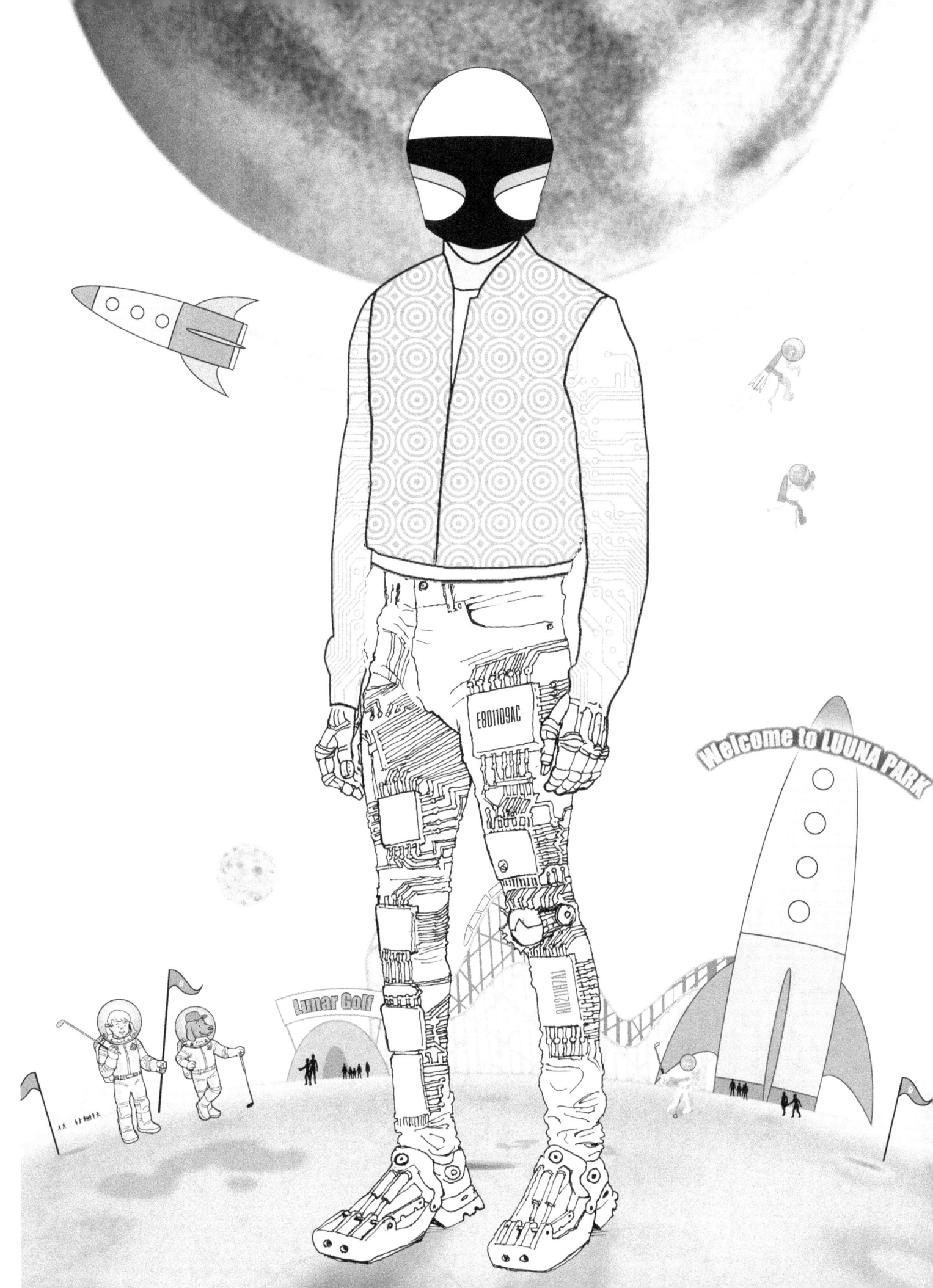

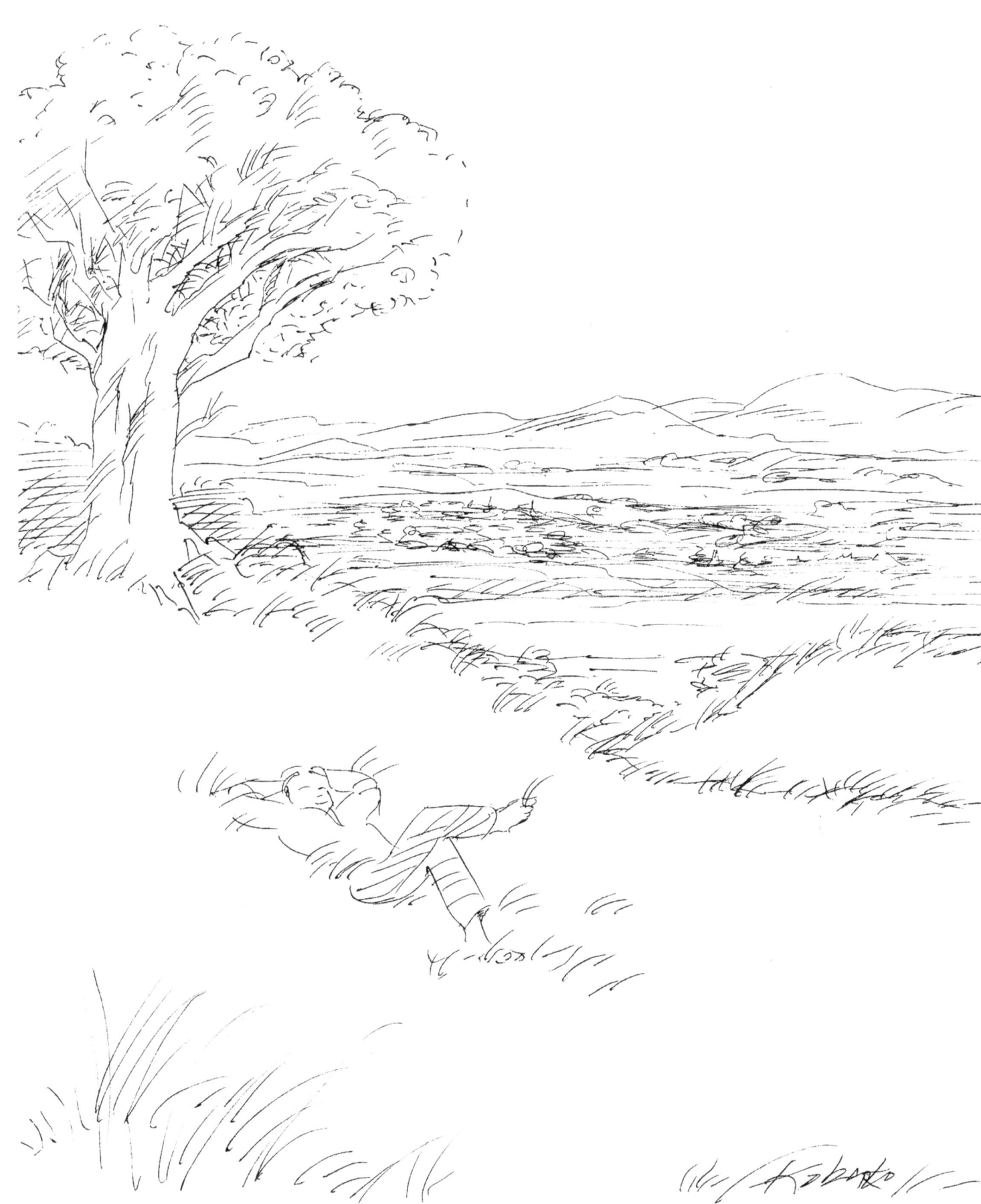

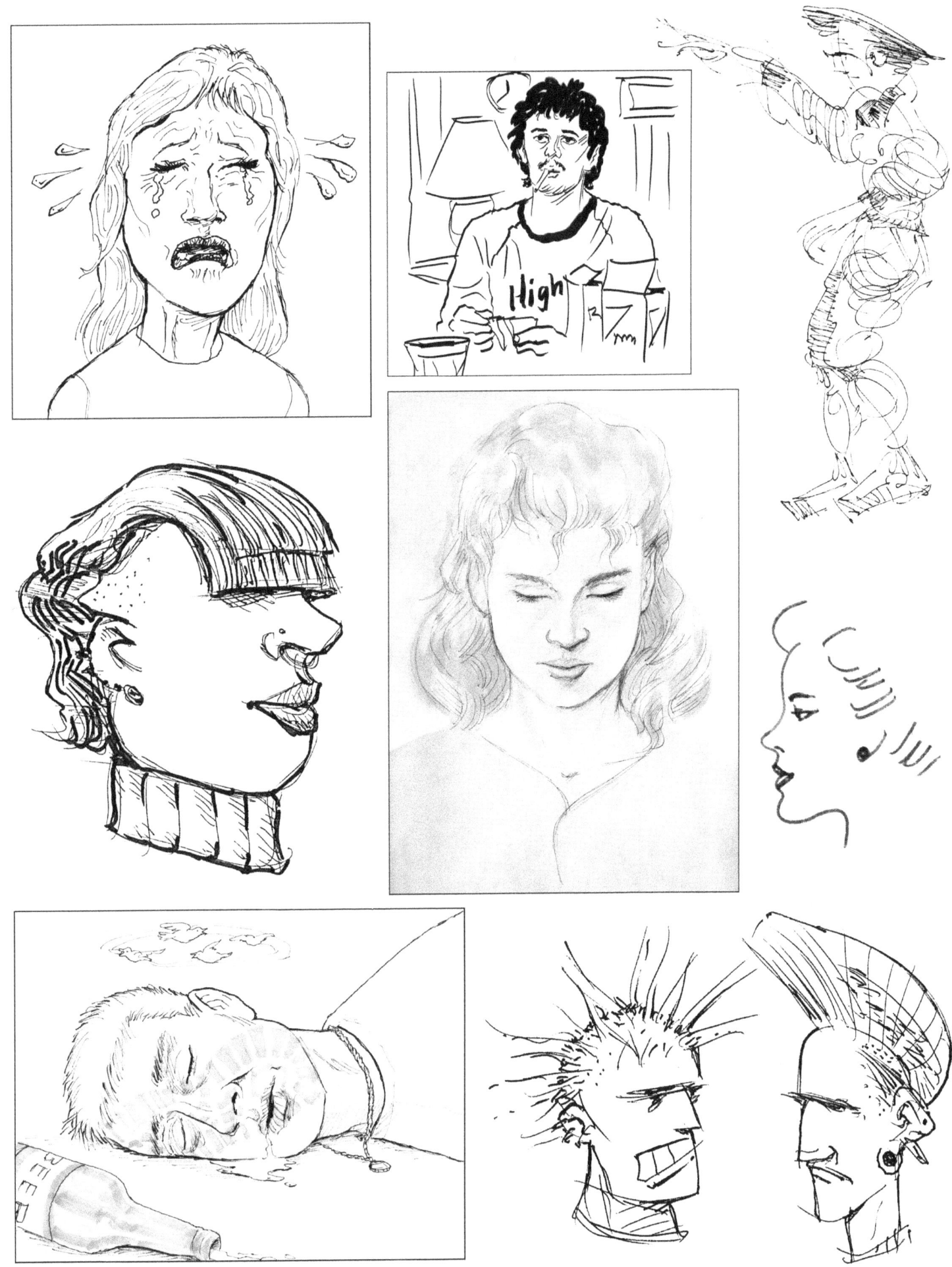

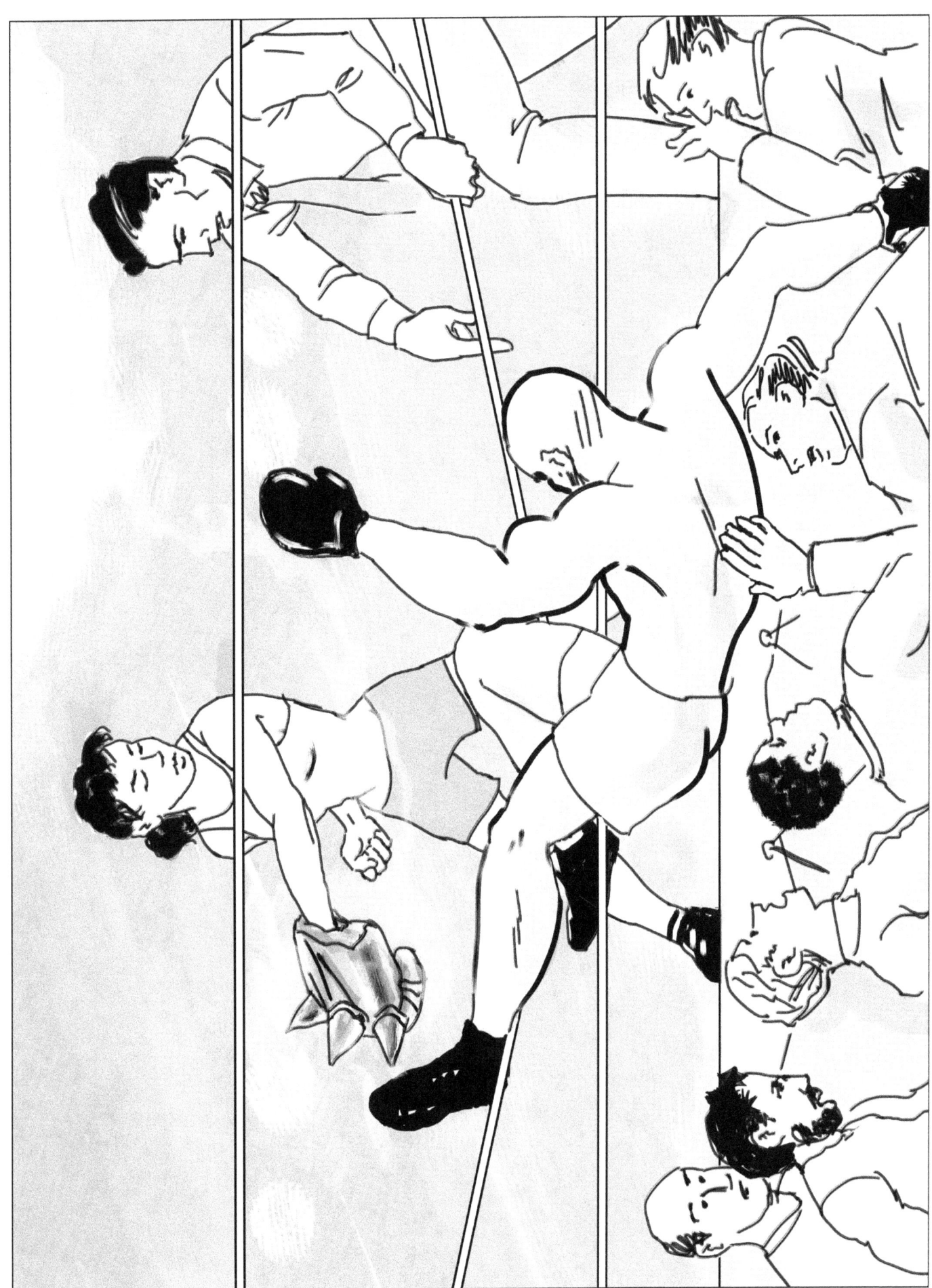

ARTIST'S TIP: Check out the work of cartoonist Wallace Wood to see one of the early influences on my work.

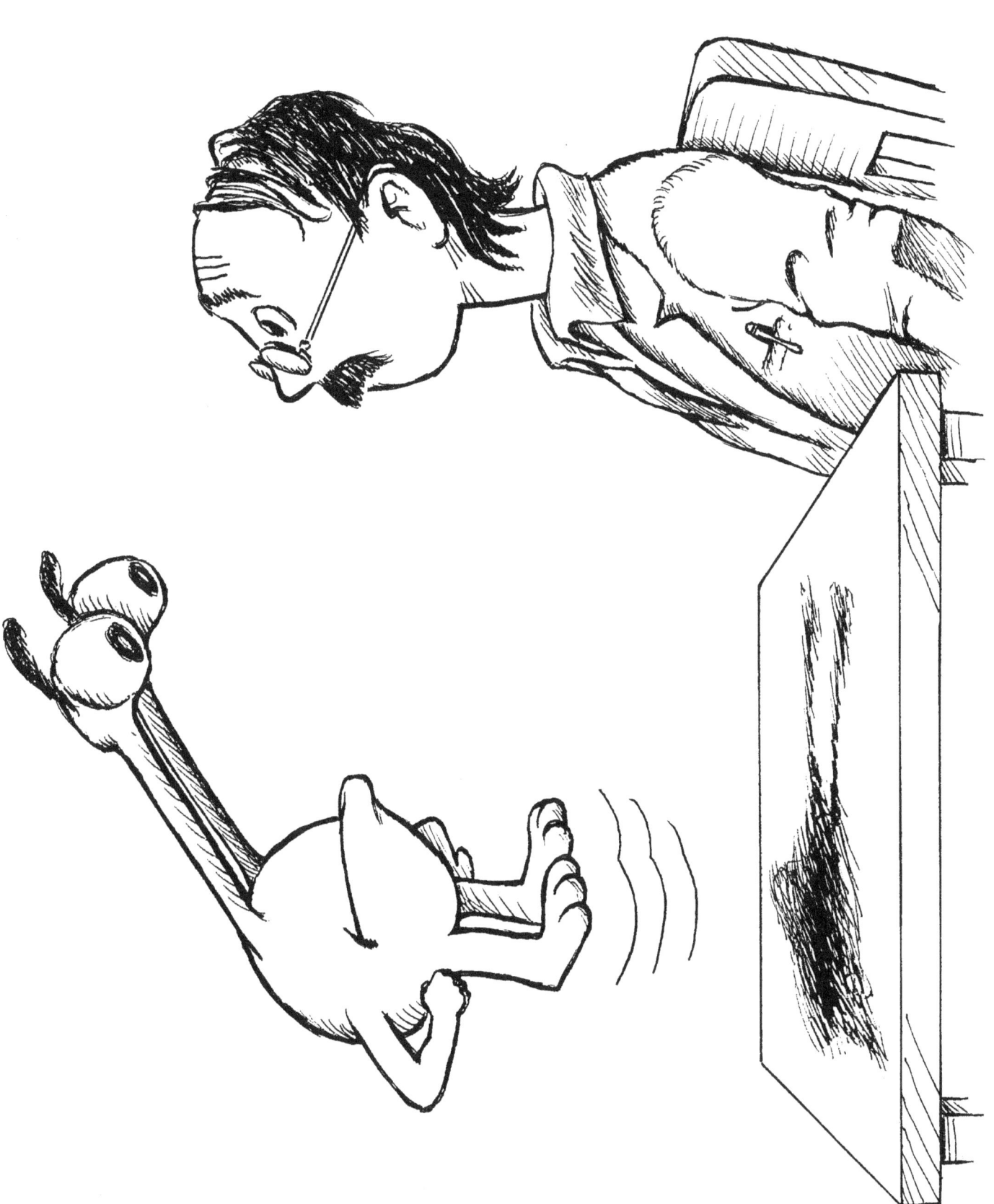

ARTIST'S TIP: To convey a gold (or other metallic) tone, I suggest using two neighboring colors (e.g. yellow and pale orange for gold, or blue and gray for silver). Leave the shiniest highlights alone, letting the white of the paper shine through. Markers may be the best way to go with this one or start lightly with color pencils, then build up the layers of opacity.

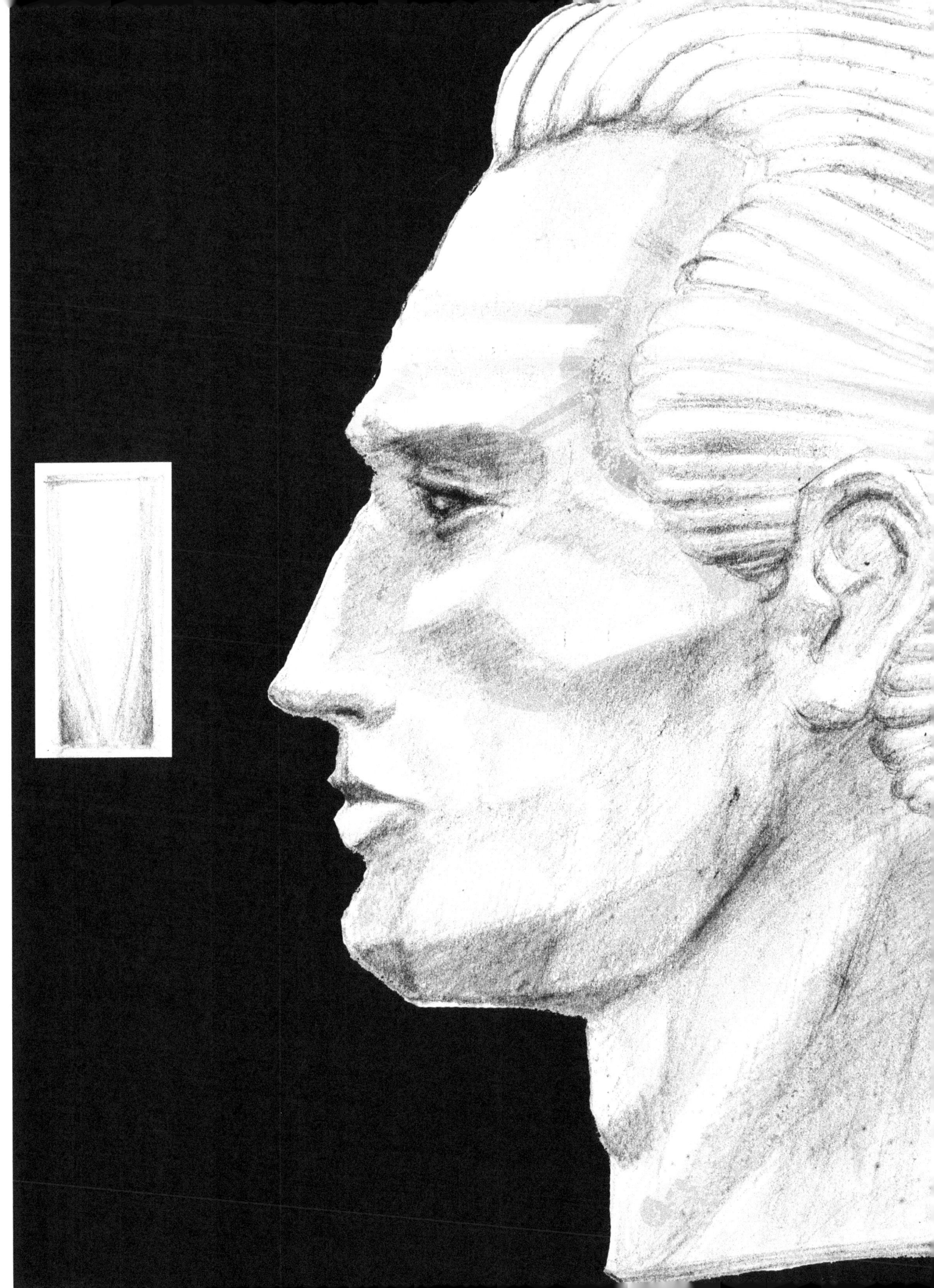

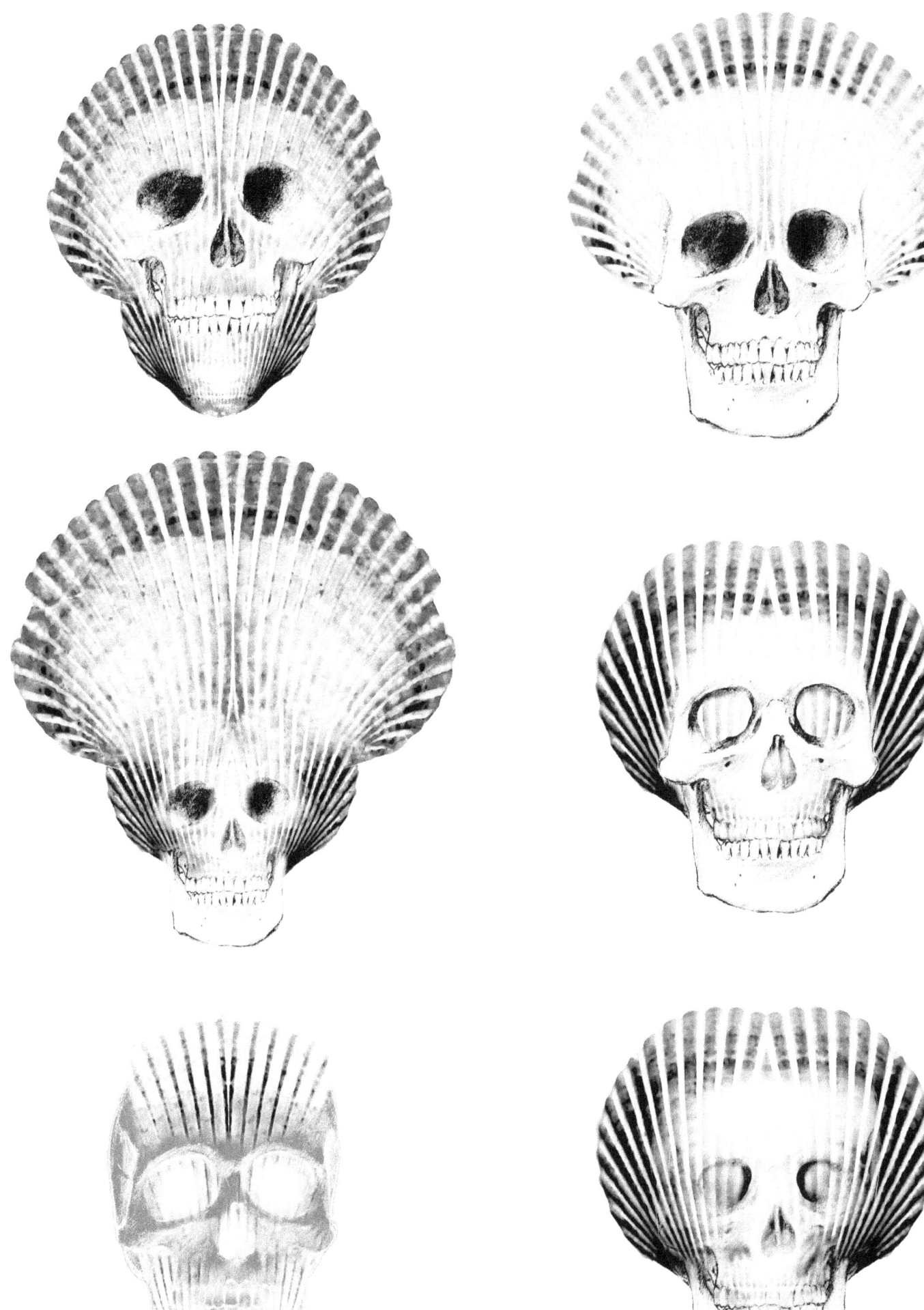

ARTIST'S TIP: Two of the masked figures have different light sources so you might work that out first, before attempting to do each respective figure. You could then adjust your shading for the other two figures to stay consistent with your light source. (If that's too confusing or limiting, disregard this advice.)

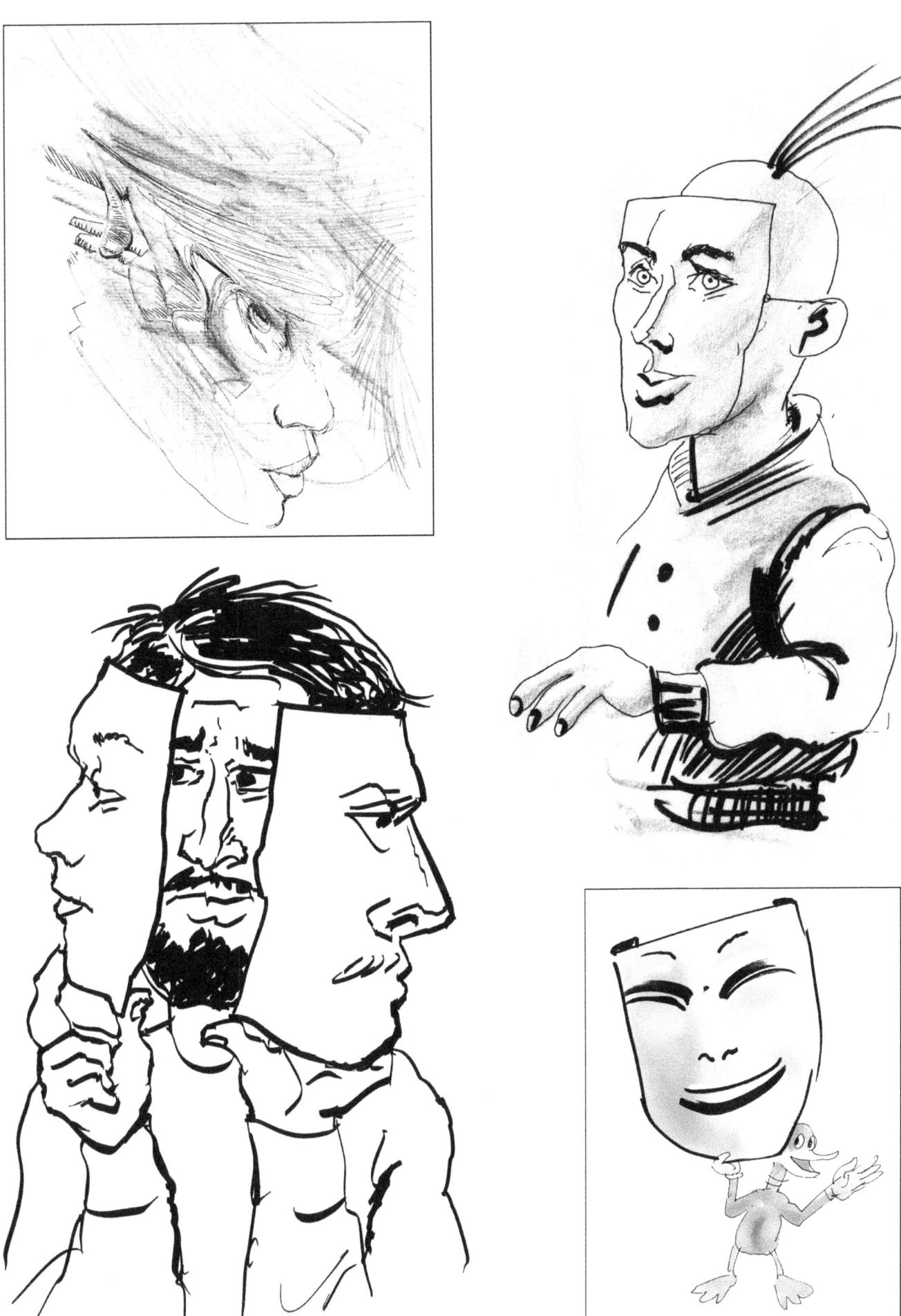

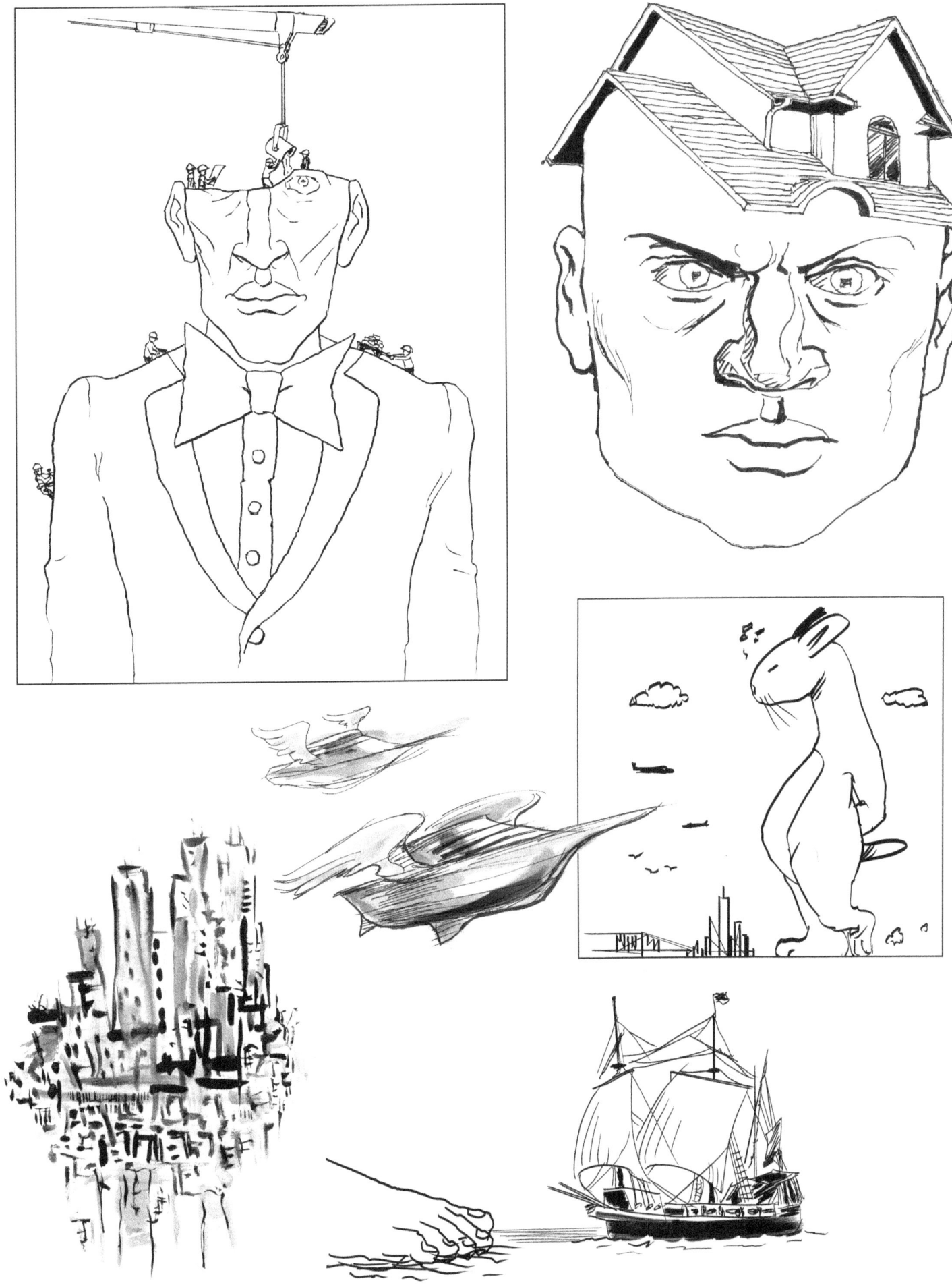

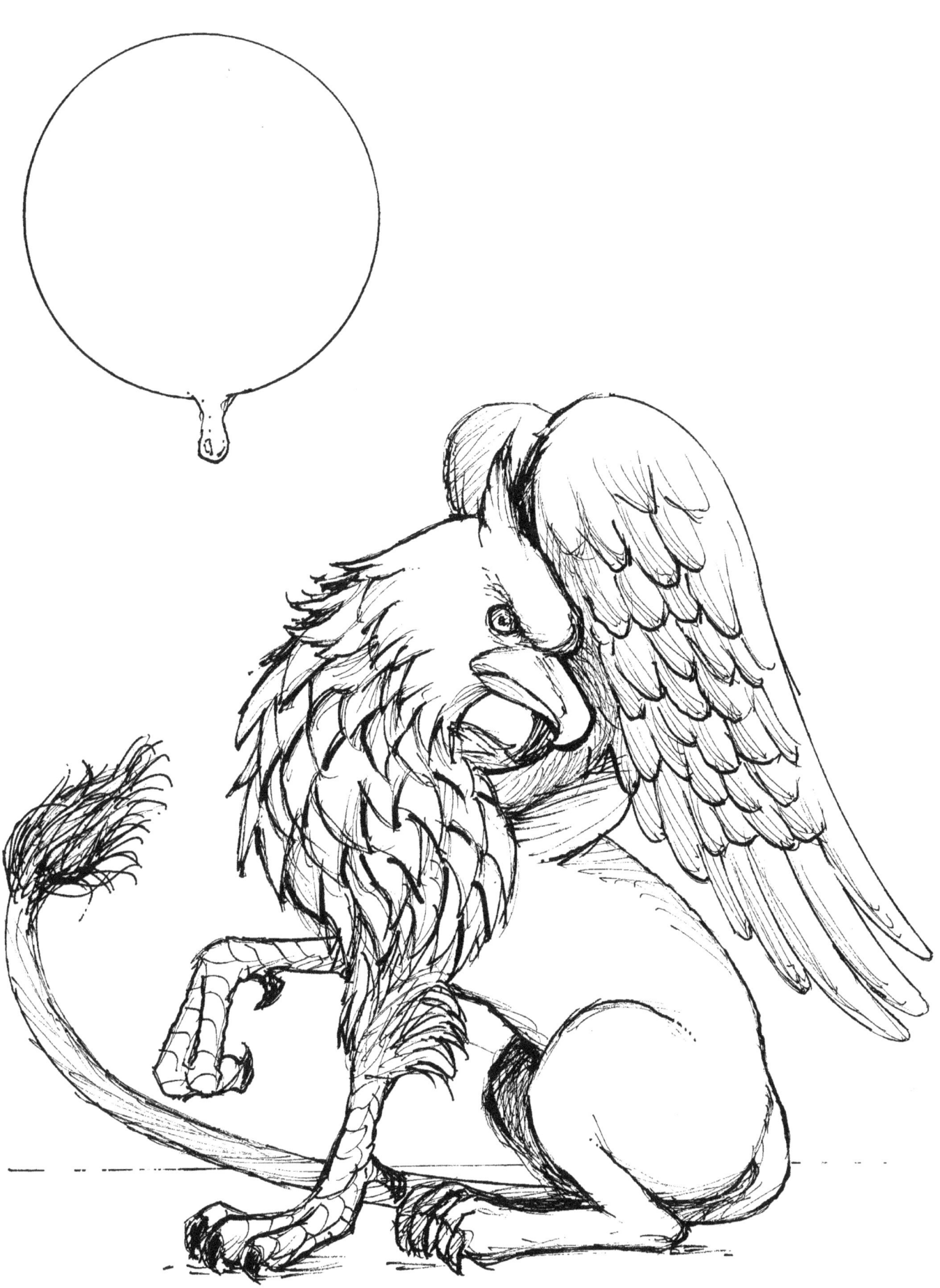

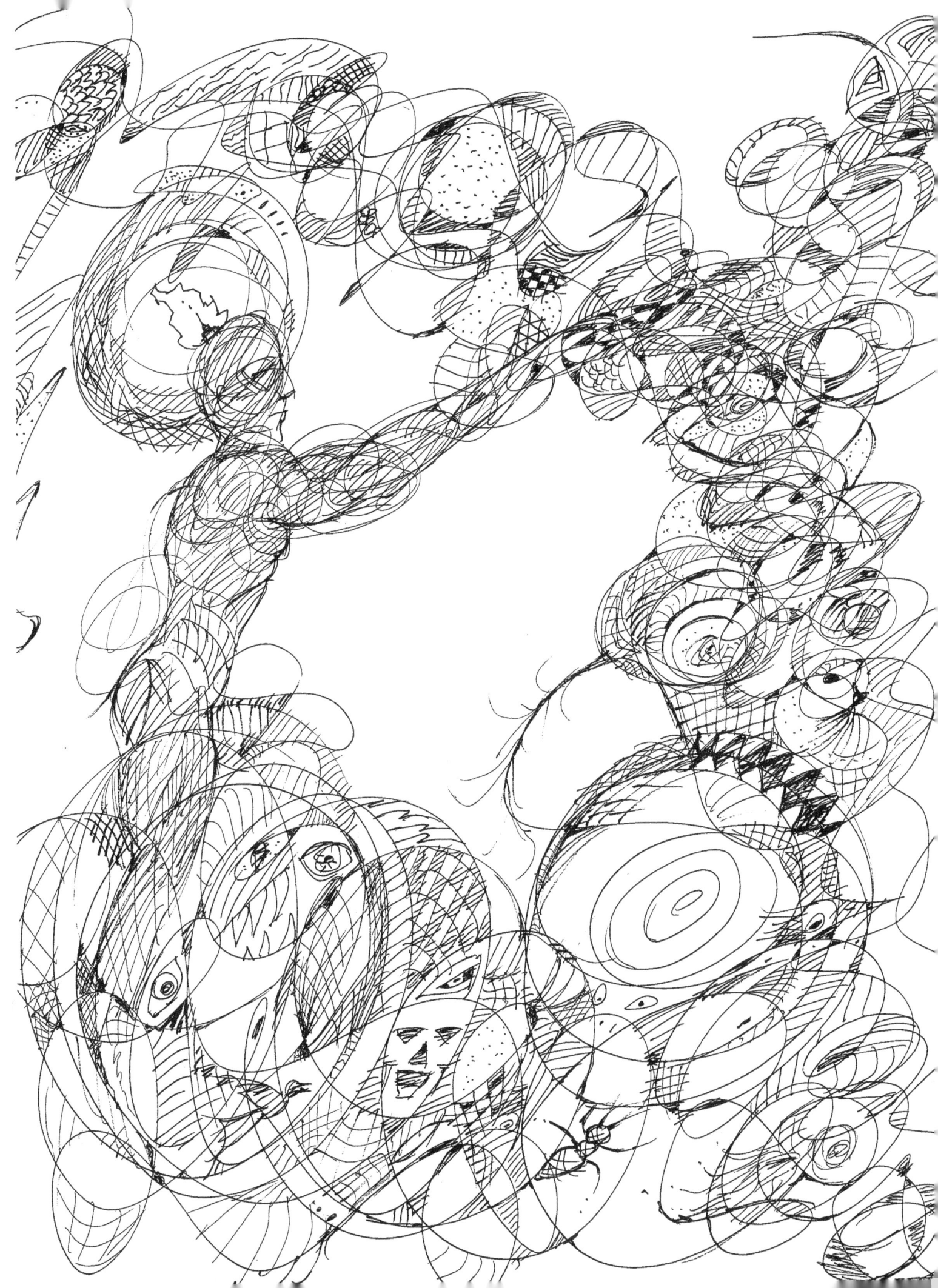

ARTIST'S TIP: Email me if you come up with any good names for these critters.

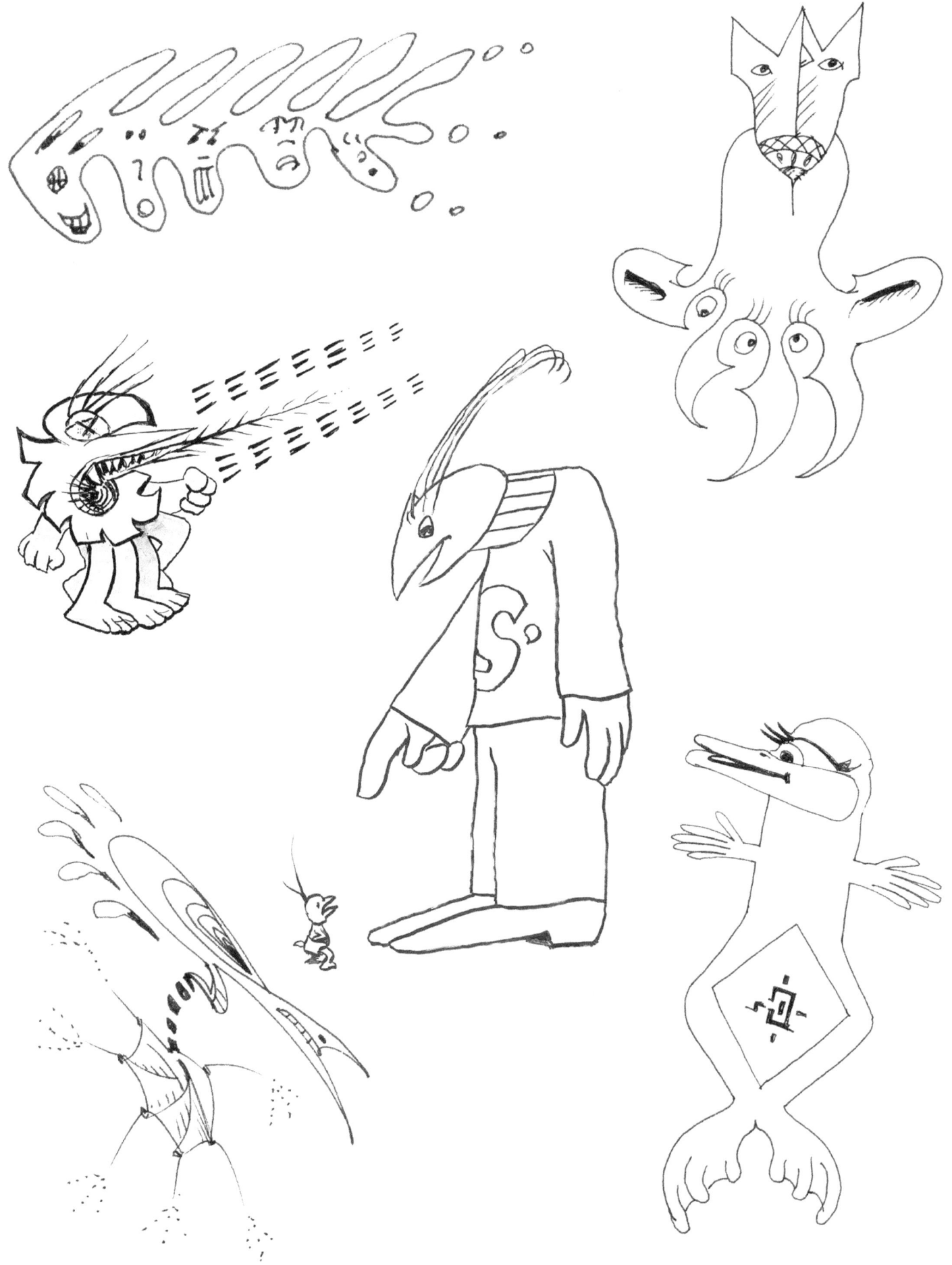

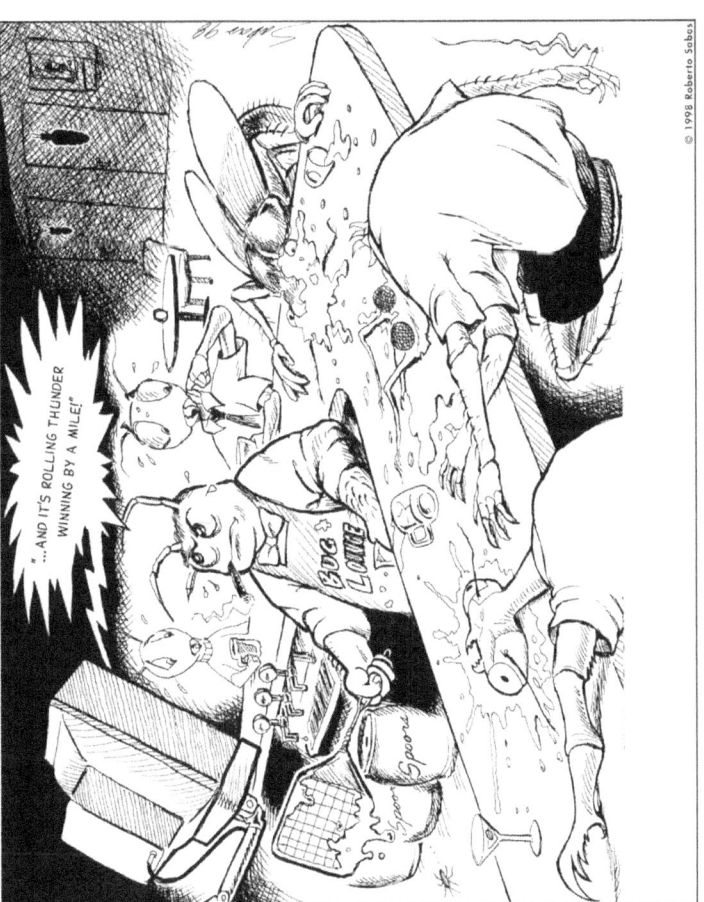

CAPTION-WRITING TIPS:

KEEP IT SHORT.
KEEP IT SIMPLE.
MAKE IT FUNNY.

READ IT TO SOMEONE...

IF NO LAUGHS,
REWRITE IT.

POLISH IT UP AND
KEEP ON WRITING
MORE GAGS!

WRITE YOUR OWN CAPTION &
SEND PHOTO OR SCAN TO:
ROBERTO.SABAS@GMAIL.COM

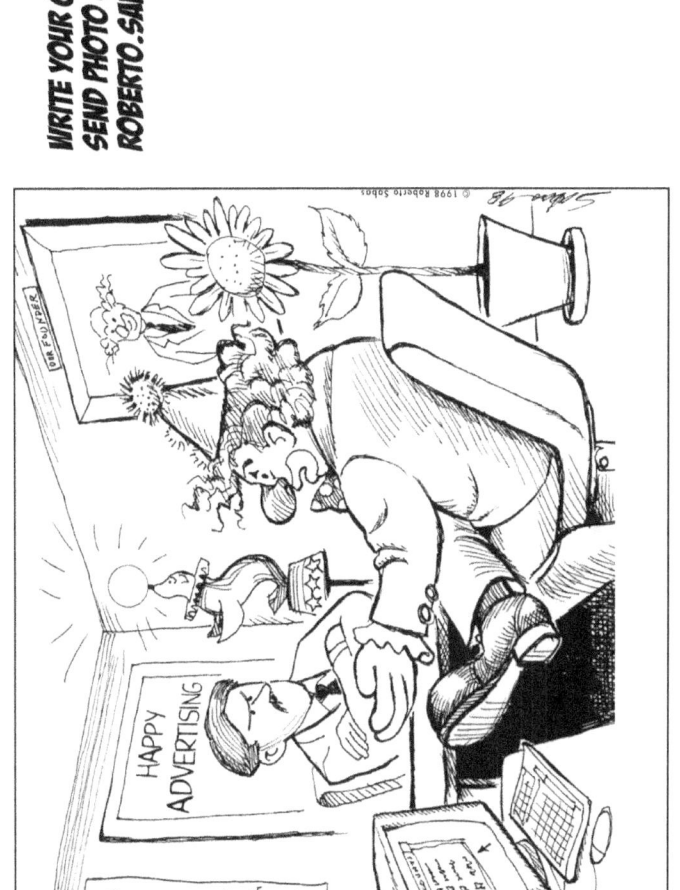

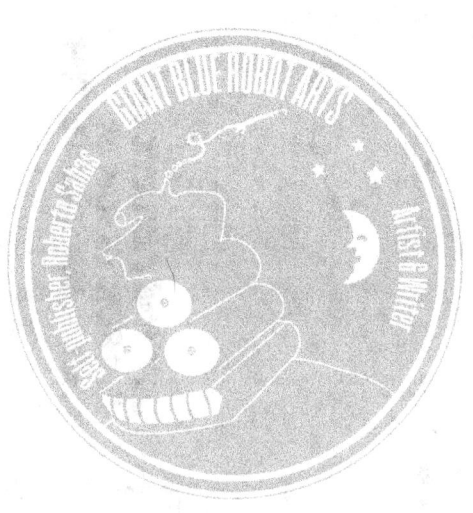